THE IDEA OF ROME
From Antiquity to the Renaissance

THE
IDEA OF ROME

From Antiquity to the Renaissance

Edited by David Thompson

ALBUQUERQUE
UNIVERSITY OF NEW MEXICO PRESS

Designed by Bruce Gentry
First Edition

CONTENTS

INTRODUCTION

"WHAT is all history," Petrarch asked with a flourish, "other than the praise of Rome?" A rhetorical exaggeration, but one containing a profound truth. It was the astonishing rise of Rome that prompted Polybius to the writing of universal—not merely local, episodic—history (indeed, the rise of Rome and its decline have been called the two great problems of historiography); the sheer duration and extent of Rome's ascendancy makes it an object of unique interest and importance; a large part of the Greek and Hebraic legacy entered the West through Roman channels (if not over Roman roads); much western law and political nomenclature (e.g., Czar, Kaiser, senator, pontiff) has been Roman; and, on a still more basic level, half the tongues of Europe (not to mention half the words on this page) descend from Latin, which was itself Europe's dominant language for the better part of two millennia, and until yesterday the liturgical language of the world's largest religious body. The study—if not the praise—of Rome is a prerequisite to any serious understanding of the development of western civilization.

In this book of readings I have tried to illuminate one important aspect of that story, by illustrating what Rome has meant to historians and poets, humanists and theologians, artists and men of letters: noble example and city of ruins; object of hatred and source of artistic inspiration; unifier of mankind and imperialist juggernaut; mistress of the world and "Niobe of nations." As Huizinga observed, "for the history of civilization every delusion or opinion of an epoch has the value of an important fact"; and nowhere is this more the case than in the study of Rome, the Eternal City which has occupied such an important place in the western imagination. No other city has cast such a spell upon men's minds, has possessed such a mystique, has generated so many potent myths.

I have accorded special emphasis to Rome's relationship with the Greek world, from which it took so much; with Christianity, which owed so much to Rome; with Gaul, which succeeded Rome as the leading cultural and political force in the western world; and with Florence, the "first modern state" (Burckhardt). The first two parts present classical Rome as it appeared to contemporaries, from a Greek historian who rationalized the Republic's conquest of his country, to a Greek sophist who eulogized the Empire of the Antonines three centuries later. The third part shows how earlier ideas—or perhaps by this time we must call them myths—about Rome flourished as the city was passing from the control of the emperors to that of the popes; and the fourth part illustrates several uses of the past, various reactions to—and inspirations drawn from—the ruins of Rome. Each part concludes with a pertinent selection from a classic of modern historiography. (These too are not entirely lacking in mythic flavor.) A special Appendix shows how Florentines of the late Middle Ages and Renaissance viewed themselves with regard to Rome.

For any one interested in pursuing the subject further, there are many relevant books and articles in English, some of which have been cited in the notes on individual texts and in a brief general bibliography (which also lists a few major works in foreign languages, and paperback editions of authors represented in this volume). Since the reader's primary interest will presumably be Polybius and company, editorial matter has been kept at a necessary minimum; but perhaps a few general observations may not be out of order at this point.

1. *Quamdiu stat Colysaeus stat et Roma; quando cadet Colysaeus cadet et Roma; quando cadet Roma cadet et mundus.*[1] The most striking idea of Rome has been the notion that it would endure until the end of time. Other cities have come and gone; but Rome so dominated men's bodies and minds, for so many centuries, that it became difficult to imagine a world without Rome. Christian polemic could readily view the new Babylon as co-extensive with the temporal world, the city of man, the realm of Satan, to pass away with the coming of Christ's kingdom. From another point of view, one might emphasize Rome's antiquity and her remarkable powers of recuperation; or her divine mission; or her freedom from the weaknesses that had afflicted mere mortal realms. Four centuries after Augustus, Claudian proclaims:

> Nor will there ever be a limit to the empire of Rome, for luxury and its attendant vices, and pride with sequent hate have brought to ruin all kingdoms else. 'Twas thus that Sparta laid low the foolish pride of Athens but to fall herself a victim to Thebes; thus that the Mede deprived the Assyrian of empire and the Persian the Mede. Macedonia subdued Persia and was herself to yield to Rome. But Rome found her strength in the oracles of the Sibyl, her vigor in the hallowed laws of Numa.[2]

2. *Moribus antiquis res stat Romana virisque.*[3] The most captivating idea of Rome has been an idealized, almost Utopian vision of the Noble Republic.[4] Roman writers of the first century B.C., *laudatores temporis acti* almost to a man, looked back nostalgically to a quasi-mythical earlier period of antique virtue, religion, simplicity and poverty, which had given way in their own age to ostentation, debauchery and and the horrors of civil war. When Saint Augustine set out to show that Rome had reached a parlous state even before the advent of

Christianity, these authors accordingly provided him with a full brief of incriminating evidence. According to Augustine, at the beginning of the fifth book of his *De Re Publica* ("On the Commonwealth") Cicero quoted the above verse of Ennius and remarked:

> This verse seems to me to have all the sententious truth-fulness of an oracle. For neither would the citizens have availed without the morality of the community, nor would the morality of the commons without outstanding men have availed either to establish or so long to maintain in vigor so grand a republic with so wide and just an empire. Accordingly, before our day, the hereditary usages formed our foremost men, and they on their part retained the usages and institutions of their fathers. But our age, receiving the republic as a *chef-d'oeuvre* of another age which has already begun to grow old, has not merely neglected to restore the colors of the original, but has not even been at the pains to preserve so much as the general outline and most outstanding features.[5]

3. *Haec est in gremium victos quae sola recepit.*[6] The most compelling idea of Rome has been that of a just mother that received the vanquished into her universal, beneficent embrace. The Roman empire antedated the Roman Empire; and in Cicero's view a radical change in the *imperium* also began in his own life-time, for after Sulla's atrocities against Roman citizens no oppression of their allies could seem wrong. But in former times, he asserts—and in subsequent times, others were to declare—the empire was maintained by "acts of service," for "wars were waged in the interest of our allies," and "the highest ambition of our magistrates and generals was to defend our provinces and allies with justice and honor." This having been the case, "our government could be called

more accurately a protectorate [*patrocinium*] of the world than a dominion."[7]

A familiar enough litany, and one that until recently carried a certain degree of conviction—at least in imperial nations like the United States, where in 1850 a southern journalist proclaimed:

We have a destiny to perform, a "manifest destiny" over all Mexico, over South America, over the West Indies and Canada. The Sandwich Islands are as necessary to our eastern as the isles of the gulf to our western commerce. The gates of the Chinese empire must be thrown down by the men from the Sacramento and the Oregon, and the haughty Japanese tramplers upon the cross be enlightened in the doctrines of republicanism and the ballot box. The eagle of the republic shall poise itself over the field of Waterloo, after tracing its flight among the gorges of the Himalaya or the Ural mountains, and a successor of Washington ascend the chair of universal empire![8]

As William Berg has observed, in discussing the school curriculum (which generally is a good guide to what a nation considers important), Rome could claim a prominent place as long as we felt she was "ours":

Martial vigor, the glory of battle, the racially justified imposition of imperium on subject peoples—these valiant dreams which Latin Classics had fostered in the Anglo-Saxon soul were applauded by a young America getting its first zesty taste of international prestige. The comprehension of Roman virtues,—its pietas, its gravitas, its amor imperii—was deemed an essential part of the moral education of our youth. This ideological orientation of Latin studies persisted even when Latin itself began to fade from the required curriculum: today as yesterday, the traditional Caesar-Cicero-Virgil sequence culminates in the breathless exegesis of these "noble" verses,

tu regere imperio populos, Romane, memento
(hae tibi erunt artes), pacisque imponere morem,
parcere subiectis et debellare superbos.

The world will not allow us to behave this way forever.[9]

Now that the sun has set somewhat on the British Empire, and the *Pax Americana* has proven itself more Pacific than pacific, our Roman forerunners begin to appear in a different light. In a brilliant series of lectures (delivered, interestingly enough, at the University of South Africa), E. Badian has summarily dismissed the notion that Roman imperial policy was governed by some moral code or lofty cultural ideal: even in the good old days, Romans showed considerably more dedication to the *utile* than to the *honestum*. But Badian accords with Cicero in one respect: the *imperium* did become more openly rapacious than ever in the first century B.C., with the annexation of Cyprus, the invasion of Parthia, and Caesar's conquest of Gaul (he reaped a huge fortune from the sale of Gallic slaves). "No administration in history," Badian concludes, "has ever devoted itself so whole-heartedly to fleecing its subjects for the private benefit of its ruling class as Rome of the last age of the Republic."[10] Another noted historian comments: "That sentence . . . will even today shock some Roman historians and some readers. Half a century ago it would have been unthinkable, at least outside Marxist circles."[11] As so often happens, a changed perspective has generated a new interpretation of the past, a revision of earlier ideas about Rome. But this does not mean that Rome will cease to figure largely in men's conceptions of western civilization; indeed, as Geoffrey Barraclough has observed, "For any one who believes in the 'relevance' or actuality of history, there is less to be gained, in the present world, from scrutin-

izing anxiously the origins of the Second World War than
from studying Caesar and the Roman revolution, a revolution
which may be paralleled sooner than we think in our own
society."[12]

1 Bede: "As long as the Colosseum stands, Rome also stands; when the
Colosseum falls, Rome also will fall; when Rome falls, the world also will
fall." Quoted by Charles Till Davis, Dante and the Idea of Rome (Oxford,
1957), p. 3. See F. G. Moore, "On Urbs Aeterna and Urbs Sacra," Transactions of the American Philological Association XXV (1894), 34-60.
2 De Consulatu Stilichonis III, 159-167 (trans. Platnauer, Loeb Classical
Library). On the philosophy of history developed by opponents of Hellenistic and Roman imperialism, see Joseph Ward Swain, "The Theory of the
Four Monarchies: Opposition History under the Roman Empire," Classical
Philology XXXV (1940), 1-21. This culminated in Orosius' Seven Books
of Histories against the Pagans (ca. 418), which for a thousand years remained a standard guide to classical history.
3 From the Annales of Ennius (239-169 B.C.): "The Roman commonwealth stands firm on a basis of good old-fashioned morality and men of
courage."
4 Cf. Clifford H. Moore, "Rome's Heroic Past in the Poems of Claudian,"
Classical Journal VI (1910-11), 108-115: "It will be be seen that almost all
those whom Claudian celebrated belonged to the period before the close
of the Punic Wars. The fall of Carthage for later generations marked the
end of Rome's heroic age. After that Roman life and action fell to mortal
plane, and only a few like Pompey and Cato were canonized" (pp. 114-
115). Cf. also Montesquieu, Considerations on the Causes of the Greatness of the Romans and their Decline, trans. David Lowenthal (Ithaca,
1968).
5 The City of God II, 21 (Dods translation). Much of Cicero's text survives
only through quotations by such Christian writers as Lactantius and
Augustine.
6 Claudian, op. cit. III, 150: " 'Tis she alone who has received the conquered
into her bosom" (even if she did have to seek them out: vincendos alio
quaesivit in orbe Britannos).
7 De Officiis ("On Moral Duties") II, viii (trans. Miller, Loeb Classical
Library).
8 Quoted by Geoffrey Barraclough, An Introduction to Contemporary History
(Pelican Book), p. 102; from R. W. van Alstyne, The Rising American
Empire (Oxford & New York, 1960), p. 152.
9 The Quest, volume I, No. 2. The lines quoted by Professor Berg, from
Anchises' injunction, conclude the second Virgilian passage in this book.
Cf. Classical Journal VI (1910-11), on Virgil's "deep and true insight into
the real mission of Rome at her ideal best—the mission of a state set to call
men from the savage, unordered and disintegrating ways of life, to organize

them under law, to conserve their achievements by custom, and to make their progress perpetual" (p. 14).

[10] Roman Imperialism in the Late Republic (Ithaca, 1968), p. 87.

[11] M. I. Finley, "A Profitable Empire," The New York Review of Books XIV, Numbers 1 & 2 (January 29, 1970), 52. For a clarification of Finley's point, see the exchange of letters in XIV, 9 (May 7, 1970), 46. There is a more sympathetic view of Roman rule in J. R. Hawthorn, The Republican Empire (London & New York, 1963) than in Finley, A History of Sicily: Ancient Sicily to the Arab Conquest (New York, 1968).

[12] The New York Review of Books XIV, 11 (June 4, 1970), 51. This is by no means a new note in Barraclough's thought: for many acute remarks on the significance of Rome, see his History in a Changing World (Oxford, 1955, 1956).

PART ONE: THE NOBLE REPUBLIC

When Fortune made us lords of all, wealth flowed,
And then we grew licentious and rude;
The soldiers' prey and rapine brought in riot;
Men took delight in jewels, houses, plate,
And scorn'd old sparing diet, and ware robes
Too light for women; Poverty (who hatch'd
Rome's greatest wits) was loath'd, and all the world
Ransack'd for gold, which breeds the world decay;
And then large limits had their butting lands;
The ground which Curius and Camillus till'd
Was stretch'd unto the fields of hinds unknown.

Lucan, *De Bello Civili* I, 160-170
(trans. Marlowe)

POLYBIUS

Born in Arcadia toward the end of the third century B.C., Polybius was the son of an eminent statesman in the Achaean League; and by 169 B.C. he had himself become Hipparch (cavalry commander) of the League. After the Roman victory at Pydna in 168 B.C. (which exterminated the Antigonid dynasty that occupied the throne of Alexander the Great in Macedon), Polybius found himself among the thousand eminent Achaeans who were accused of less than full loyalty to Rome, summoned to Italy, and kept there sixteen years without a trial. However, Polybius was fortunate enough to become friendly with Scipio Aemilianus (son of the Roman commander at Pydna), whose circle he joined and whom he accompanied on missions outside the country. He witnessed the fall of Carthage in 146 B.C.; and after the Romans went on to destroy Carthage in the same year, Polybius acted as intermediary between Achaea and Rome, in recognition of which service several cities erected statues to him.

The Histories describe the course of events from the outbreak of the First Punic War in 264 B.C. through the destruction of Carthage and Corinth. Polybius was apparently still working on them at the time of his death about 120 B.C.

See J. B. Bury, Ancient Greek Historians (London, 1909; reprinted New York, 1958); and T. R. Glover, "Polybius," Cambridge Ancient History VIII (1930), 1-24.

From The Histories of Polybius, trans. Evelyn S. Shuckburgh (London & New York: Macmillan, 1889; reprinted with a new introduction by F. W. Walbank, Indiana University Press: Bloomington, 1962).

THE UNIQUENESS OF ROME
(*Histories* I, 1-4)

HAD the praise of History been passed over by former Chron-
iclers it would perhaps have been incumbent upon me to urge
the choice and special study of records of this sort, as the
readiest means men can have to correcting their knowledge of
the past. But my predecessors have not been sparing in this
respect. They have all begun and ended, so to speak, by en-
larging on this theme: asserting again and again that the study
of History is in the truest sense an education, and a training
for political life; and that the most instructive, or rather the
only, method of learning to bear with dignity the vicissitudes
of fortune is to recall the catastrophes of others. It is evident,
therefore, that no one need think it his duty to repeat what
has been said by many, and said well. Least of all myself: for
the surprising nature of the events which I have undertaken
to relate is in itself sufficient to challenge and stimulate the
attention of every one, old or young, to the study of my work.
Can any one be so indifferent or idle as not to care to know by
what means, and under what kind of polity, almost the whole
inhabited world was conquered and brought under the
dominion of the single city of Rome, and that too within a
period of not quite fifty-three years? Or who again can be so
completely absorbed in other subjects of contemplation or
study, as to think any of them superior in importance to the
accurate understanding of an event for which the past affords
no precedent?

We shall best show how marvellous and vast our subject is
by comparing the most famous Empires which preceded, and
which have been the favorite themes of historians, and mea-

suring them with the superior greatness of Rome. There are but three that deserve even to be so compared and measured: and they are these. The Persians for a certain length of time were possessed of a great empire and dominion. But every time they ventured beyond the limits of Asia, they found not only their empire, but their own existence also in danger. The Lacedaemonians, after contending for supremacy in Greece for many generations, when they did get it, held it without dispute for barely twelve years.[1] The Macedonians obtained dominion in Europe from the lands bordering on the Adriatic to the Danube,—which after all is but a small fraction of this continent,—and, by the destruction of the Persian Empire, they afterwards added to that the dominion of Asia. And yet, though they had the credit of having made themselves masters of a larger number of countries and states than any people had ever done, they still left the greater half of the inhabited world in the hands of others. They never so much as thought of attempting Sicily, Sardinia, or Libya: and as to Europe, to speak the plain truth, they never even knew of the most warlike tribes of the West. The Roman conquest, on the other hand, was not partial. Nearly the whole inhabited world was reduced by them to obedience: and they left behind them an empire not to be paralleled in the past or rivalled in the future. Students will gain from my narrative a clearer view of the whole story, and of the numerous and important advantages which such exact record of events offers.

My History begins in the 140th Olympiad.[2] The events from which it starts are these. In Greece, what is called the Social war: the first waged by Philip, son of Demetrius and father of Perseus, in league with the Achaeans against the Aetolians. In Asia, the war for the possession of Coele-Syria which Antiochus and Ptolemy Philopator carried on against each other. In Italy, Libya, and their neighborhood, the conflict between Rome and Carthage, generally called the Han-

nibalian war. My work thus begins where that of Aratus of
Sicyon leaves off. Now up to this time the world's history had
been, so to speak, a series of disconnected transactions, as
widely separated in their origin and results as in their localities.
But from this time forth History becomes a connected whole:
the affairs of Italy and Libya are involved with those of Asia
and Greece, and the tendency of all is to unity. This is why I
have fixed upon this era as the starting-point of my work. For
it was their victory over the Carthaginians in this war, and
their conviction that thereby the most difficult and most
essential step towards universal empire had been taken, which
encouraged the Romans for the first time to stretch out their
hands upon the rest, and to cross with an army into Greece
and Asia.

Now, had the states that were rivals for universal empire
been familiarly known to us, no reference perhaps to their
previous history would have been necessary, to show the
purpose and the forces with which they approached an undertaking of this nature and magnitude. But the fact is that the
majority of the Greeks have no knowledge of the previous
constitution, power, or achievements either of Rome or
Carthage. I therefore concluded that it was necessary to prefix
this and the next book to my History. I was anxious that no
one, when fairly embarked upon my actual narrative, should
feel at a loss, and have to ask what were the designs entertained
by the Romans, or the forces and means at their disposal, that
they entered upon those undertakings, which did in fact lead
to their becoming masters of land and sea everywhere in our
part of the world. I wished, on the contrary, that these books
of mine, and the prefatory sketch which they contained, might
make it clear that the resources they started with justified their
original idea, and sufficiently explained their final success in
grasping universal empire and dominion.

There is this analogy between the plan of my History and

the marvellous spirit of the age with which I have to deal. Just as Fortune made almost all the affairs of the world incline in one direction, and forced them to converge upon one and the same point; so it is my task as an historian to put before my readers a compendious view of the part played by Fortune in bringing about her general purpose. It was this peculiarity which originally challenged my attention, and determined me on undertaking this work. And combined with this was the fact that no writer of our time has undertaken a general history. Had any one done so my ambition in this direction would have been much diminished. But, in point of fact, I notice that by far the greater number of historians concern themselves with isolated wars and the incidents that accompany them: while as to a general and comprehensive scheme of events, their date, origin, and catastrophe, no one as far as I know has undertaken to examine it. I thought it, therefore, distinctly my duty neither to pass by myself, nor allow any one else to pass by, without full study, a characteristic specimen of the dealings of Fortune at once brilliant and instructive in the highest degree. For fruitful as Fortune is in change, and constantly as she is producing dramas in the life of men, yet never assuredly before this did she work such a marvel, or act such a drama, as that which we have witnessed. And of this we cannot obtain a comprehensive view from writers of mere episodes. It would be as absurd to expect to do so as for a man to imagine that he has learnt the shape of the whole world, its entire arrangement and order, because he has visited one after the other the most famous cities in it; or perhaps merely examined them in separate pictures. That would be indeed absurd: and it has always seemed to me that men, who are persuaded that they get a competent view of universal from episodical history, are very like persons who should see the limbs of some body, which had once been living and beautiful, scattered and remote; and should imagine that to be quite as

good as actually beholding the activity and beauty of the
living creature itself. But if some one could there and then
reconstruct the animal once more, in the perfection of its
beauty and the charm of its vitality, and could display it to the
same people, they would beyond doubt confess that they had
been far from conceiving the truth, and had been little better
than dreamers. For indeed some idea of a whole may be got
from a part, but an accurate knowledge and clear comprehension cannot. Wherefore we must conclude that episodical
history contributes exceedingly little to the familiar knowledge
and secure grasp of universal history. While it is only by the
combination and comparison of the separate parts of the
whole,—by observing their likeness and their difference,—that
a man can attain his object: can obtain a view at once clear
and complete; and thus secure both the profit and the delight
of History.

[1] 405-394 B.C.
[2] 220-217 B.C.

COMPARISON WITH SPARTA
AND CARTHAGE
(*Histories* VI, 48-56)

. . . NOW it seems to me that for securing unity among the
citizens, for safe-guarding the Laconian territory, and preserving the liberty of Sparta inviolate, the legislation and provisions of Lycurgus were so excellent, that I am forced to
regard his wisdom as something superhuman. For the equality

of landed possessions, the simplicity in their food, and the practice of taking it in common, which he established, were well calculated to secure morality in private life and to prevent civil broils in the State; as also their training in the endurance of labors and dangers to make men brave and noble minded: but when both these virtues, courage and high morality, are combined in one soul or in one state, vice will not easily spring from such a soil, nor will such men easily be overcome by their enemies. By constructing his constitution therefore in this spirit, and of these elements, he secured two blessings to the Spartans,—safety for their territory, and a lasting freedom for themselves long after he was gone. He appears however to have made no one provision whatever, particular or general, for the acquisition of the territory of their neighbors; or for the assertion of their supremacy; or, in a word, for any policy of aggrandizement at all. What he had still to do was to impose such a necessity, or create such a spirit among the citizens, that, as he had succeeded in making their individual lives independent and simple, the public character of the state should also become independent and moral. But the actual fact is, that, though he made them the most disinterested and sober-minded men in the world, as far as their own ways of life and their national institutions were concerned, he left them in regard to the rest of Greece ambitious, eager for supremacy, and encroaching in the highest degree.

For in the first place is it not notorious that they were nearly the first Greeks to cast a covetous eye upon the territory of their neighbors, and that accordingly they waged a war of subjugation on the Messenians? In the next place is it not related in all histories that in their dogged obstinacy they bound themselves with an oath never to desist from the siege of Messene until they had taken it? And lastly it is known to all that in their efforts for supremacy in Greece they submitted to do the bidding of those whom they had once conquered in

war. For when the Persians invaded Greece, they conquered
them, as champions of the liberty of the Greeks; yet when the
invaders had retired and fled, they betrayed the cities of Greece
into their hands by the peace of Antalcides, for the sake of
getting money to secure their supremacy over the Greeks.[1] It
was then that the defect in their constitution was rendered
apparent. For as long as their ambition was confined to governing their immediate neighbors, or even the Peloponnesians
only, they were content with the resources and supplies provided by Laconia itself, having all material of war ready to
hand, and being able without much expenditure of time to
return home or convey provisions with them. But directly
they took in hand to despatch naval expeditions, or to go on
campaigns by land outside the Peloponnese, it was evident
that neither their iron currency, nor their use of crops for
payment in kind, would be able to supply them with what
they lacked if they abided by the legislation of Lycurgus; for
such undertakings required money universally current, and
goods from foreign countries. Thus they were compelled to
wait humbly at Persian doors, impose tribute on islanders, and
exact contributions from all the Greeks: knowing that, if they
abided by the laws of Lycurgus, it was impossible to advance
any claims upon any outside power at all, much less upon the
supremacy in Greece.

My object, then, in this digression is to make it manifest by
actual facts that, for guarding their own country with absolute
safety, and for preserving their own freedom, the legislation of
Lycurgus was entirely sufficient; and for those who are content
with these objects we must concede that there neither exists,
nor ever has existed, a constitution and civil order preferable
to that of Sparta. But if any one is seeking aggrandizement,
and believes that to be a leader and ruler and despot of numerous subjects, and to have all looking and turning to him, is

a finer thing than that,—in this point of view we must acknowledge that the Spartan constitution is deficient, and that of Rome superior and better constituted for obtaining power. And this has been proved by actual facts. For when the Lacedaemonians strove to possess themselves of the supremacy in Greece, it was not long before they brought their own freedom itself into danger. Whereas the Romans, after obtaining supreme power over the Italians themselves, soon brought the whole world under their rule,—in which achievement the abundance and availability of their supplies largely contributed to their success.

Now the Carthaginian constitution seems to me originally to have been well contrived in these most distinctively important particulars. For they had kings, and the Gerusia had the powers of an aristocracy, and the multitude were supreme in such things as affected them; and on the whole the adjustment of its several parts was very like that of Rome and Sparta.[2] But about the period of its entering on the Hannibalian war the political state of Carthage was on the decline, that of Rome improving. For whereas there is in every body, or polity, or business a natural stage of growth, zenith, and decay; and whereas everything in them is at its best at the zenith; we may thereby judge of the difference between these two constitutions as they existed at that period. For exactly so far as the strength and prosperity of Carthage preceded that of Rome in point of time, by so much was Carthage then past its prime, while Rome was exactly at its zenith, as far as its political constitution was concerned. In Carthage therefore the influence of the people in the policy of the state had already risen to be supreme, while at Rome the Senate was at the height of its power: and so, as in the one measures were deliberated upon by the many, in the other by the best men, the policy of the Romans in all public undertakings proved the stronger; on which account, though they met with capital disasters, by force of prudent counsels they finally conquered the Carthaginians in the war.

If we look however at separate details, for instance at the provisions for carrying on a war, we shall find that whereas for a naval expedition the Carthaginians are the better trained and prepared,—as it is only natural with a people with whom it has been hereditary for many generations to practise this craft, and to follow the seaman's trade above all nations in the world,—yet, in regard to military service on land, the Romans train themselves to a much higher pitch than the Carthaginians. The former bestow their whole attention upon this department: whereas the Carthaginians wholly neglect their infantry, though they do take some slight interest in the cavalry. The reason of this is that they employ foreign mercenaries, the Romans native and citizen levies. It is in this point that the latter polity is preferable to the former. They have their hopes of freedom ever resting on the courage of mercenary troops: the Romans on the valor of their own citizens and the aid of their allies. The result is that even if the Romans have suffered a defeat at first, they renew the war with undiminished forces, which the Carthaginians cannot do. For, as the Romans are fighting for country and children, it is impossible for them to relax the fury of their struggle; but they persist with obstinate resolution until they have overcome their enemies. What has happened in regard to their navy is an instance in point. In skill the Romans are much behind the Carthaginians, as I have already said; yet the upshot of the whole naval war has been a decided triumph for the Romans, owing to the valor of their men. For although nautical science contributes largely to success in sea-fights, still it is the courage of the marines that turns the scale most decisively in favor of victory. The fact is that Italians as a nation are by nature superior to Phoenicians and Libyans both in physical strength and courage; but still their habits also do much to inspire the youth with enthusiasm for such exploits. One example will be sufficient of the pains taken by the Roman state to turn out men ready to endure anything to win a reputation in their country for valor.

Whenever one of their illustrious men dies, in the course of his funeral, the body with all its paraphernalia is carried into the forum to the Rostra, as a raised platform there is called, and sometimes is propped upright upon it so as to be conspicuous, or, more rarely, is laid upon it. Then with all the people standing around, his son, if he has left one of full age and he is there, or, failing him, one of his relations, mounts the Rostra and delivers a speech concerning the virtues of the deceased, and the successful exploits performed by him in his lifetime. By these means the people are reminded of what has been done, and made to see it with their own eyes,—not only such as were engaged in the actual transactions but those also who were not;—and their sympathies are so deeply moved, that the loss appears not to be confined to the actual mourners, but to be a public one affecting the whole people. After the burial and all the usual ceremonies have been performed, they place the likeness of the deceased in the most conspicuous spot in his house, surmounted by a wooden canopy or shrine. This likeness consists of a mask made to represent the deceased with extraordinary fidelity both in shape and color. These likenesses they display at public sacrifices adorned with much care. And when any illustrious member of the family dies, they carry these masks to the funeral, putting them on men whom they thought as like the originals as possible in height and other personal peculiarities. And these substitutes assume clothes according to the rank of the person represented: if he was a consul or praetor, a toga with purple stripes; if a censor, whole purple; if he had also celebrated a triumph or performed any exploit of that kind, a toga embroidered with gold. These representatives also ride themselves in chariots, while the fasces and axes, and all the other customary insignia of the particular offices, lead the way, according to the dignity of the rank in the state enjoyed by the deceased in his life-time; and on arriving at the Rostra they all take their seats on ivory chairs in their order. There could not easily be a more inspiring spectacle than this for a young man of noble ambi-tions and virtuous aspirations. For can we conceive any one to be unmoved at the sight of all the likenesses collected to-gether of the men who have earned glory, all as it were living and breathing? Or what could be a more glorious spectacle?

Besides the speaker over the body about to be buried, after having finished the panegyric of this particular person, starts upon the others whose representatives are present, beginning with the most ancient, and recounts the successes and achieve-ments of each. By this means the glorious memory of brave men is continually renewed; the fame of those who have per-formed any noble deed is never allowed to die; and the renown of those who have done good service to their country becomes a matter of common knowledge to the multitude, and part of the heritage of posterity. But the chief benefit of the ceremony is that it inspires young men to shrink from no exertion for the general welfare, in the hope of obtaining the glory which awaits the brave. And what I say is confirmed by this fact. Many Romans have volunteered to decide a whole battle by single combat; not a few have deliberately accepted certain death, some in time of war to secure the safety of the rest, some in time of peace to preserve the safety of the common-wealth. There have also been instances of men in office put-ting their own sons to death, in defiance of every custom and law, because they rated the interests of their country higher than those of natural ties even with their nearest and dearest. There are many stories of this kind, related of many men in

Roman history; but one will be enough for our present purpose; and I will give the name as an instance to prove the truth of my words.

The story goes that Horatius Cocles, while fighting with two enemies at the head of the bridge over the Tiber, which is the entrance to the city on the north, seeing a large body of men advancing to support his enemies, and fearing that they would force their way into the city, turned round, and shouted to those behind him to hasten back to the other side and break down the bridge. They obeyed him: and whilst they were breaking the bridge, he remained at his post receiving numerous wounds, and checked the progress of the enemy: his opponents being panic stricken, not so much by his strength as by the audacity with which he held his ground. When the bridge had been broken down, the attack of the enemy was stopped; and Cocles then threw himself into the river with his armor on and deliberately sacrificed his life,[3] because he valued the safety of his country and his own future reputation more highly than his present life, and the years of existence that remained to him. Such is the enthusiasm and emulation for noble deeds that are engendered among the Romans by their customs.

Again the Roman customs and principles regarding money transactions are better than those of the Carthaginians. In the view of the latter nothing is disgraceful that makes for gain; with the former nothing is more disgraceful than to receive bribes and to make profit by improper means. For they regard wealth obtained from unlawful transactions to be as much a subject of reproach, as a fair profit from the most unquestioned source is of commendation. A proof of the fact is this. The Carthaginians obtain office by open bribery, but among the Romans the penalty for it is death. With such a radical difference, therefore, between the rewards offered to virtue among the two peoples, it is natural that the ways adopted for obtaining them should be different also.

But the most important difference for the better which the Roman commonwealth appears to me to display is in their religious beliefs. For I conceive that what in other nations is looked upon as a reproach, I mean the scrupulous fear of the gods, is the very thing which keeps the Roman commonwealth together. To such an extraordinary height is this carried among them, both in private and public business, that nothing could exceed it. Many people might think this unaccountable; but in my opinion their object is to use it as a check upon the common people.[4] If it were possible to form a state wholly of philosophers, such a custom would perhaps be unnecessary. But seeing that every multitude is fickle, and full of lawless desires, unreasoning anger, and violent passion, the only resource is to keep them in check by mysterious terrors and scenic effects of this sort.[5] Wherefore, to my mind, the ancients were not acting without purpose or at random, when they brought in among the vulgar those opinions about the gods, and the belief in the punishments in Hades: much rather do I think that men nowadays are acting rashly and foolishly in rejecting them. This is the reason why, apart from anything else, Greek statesmen, if entrusted with a single talent, though protected by ten checking-clerks, as many seals, and twice as many witnesses, yet cannot be induced to keep faith: whereas among the Romans, in their magistracies and embassies, men have the handling of a great amount of money, and yet from pure respect to their oath keep their faith intact. And, again, in other nations it is a rare thing to find a man who keeps his hands out of the public purse, and is entirely pure in such matters; but among the Romans it is a rare thing to detect a man in the act of committing such a crime. . . .[6]

1 The Battle of Plataea took place in 479 B.C., the Peace of Antalcides in 387 B.C.

2 In Polybius' view, the strength of the Roman constitution, with its regard for "equality and equilibrium," lay in a balance of powers: ". . . no one could say for certain, not even a native, whether the constitution as a whole were an aristocracy or democracy or despotism. And no wonder: for if we confine our observation to the power of the Consuls we should be inclined to regard it as despotic; if on that of the Senate, as aristocratic; and if finally one looks at the power possessed by the people, it would seem a clear case of a democracy" (VI, 11). See K. von Fritz, *The Theory of the Mixed Constitution in Antiquity* (New York, 1954).

3 In Livy (II, 10) Horatius succeeds in reaching the bank alive.

4 Cf. Livy I, 18-21 (on Numa's religious institutions), and Gibbon's remark about a later period: "The various modes of worship which prevailed in the Roman world were all considered by the people as equally true; by the philosopher as equally false; and by the magistrate as equally useful."

5 Lucretius later wrote his *De Rerum Natura* to dispel precisely such religious fears.

6 However, in his recapitulation (VI, 57) Polybius warns about the baneful effects of wealth; and writing of his own times he asserts: "Some had wasted their energies on favorite youths; others on mistresses; and a great many on banquets enlivened with poetry and wine, and all the extravagant expenditure which they entailed, having quickly caught during the war with Perseus the dissoluteness of Greek manners in this respect. And to such monstrous lengths had this debauchery gone among the young men, that many of them had given a talent for a young favorite. This dissoluteness had as it were burst into flame at this period: in the first place, from the prevalent idea that, owing to the destruction of the Macedonian monarchy, universal dominion was now secured to them beyond dispute; and in the second place, from the immense difference made, both in public and private wealth and splendor, by the importation of the riches of Macedonia into Rome" (XXXII, 11).

CICERO

Although he is probably best known today as an orator, historically Cicero (106-43 B.C.) has been most important for his philosophical works, most of which he wrote in 45 and 44 B.C. to provide himself consolation and occupation during the difficult years following his divorce, the failure of his second marriage, and the death of his beloved daughter Tullia.

Now that Pompey had been defeated by Caesar, and free oratory was no longer possible, Cicero hoped to do his countrymen a service by writing philosophy in Latin for the general reader. As a young man (79-77 B.C.) he had studied with Greek philosophers and established a friendship with the Stoic Posidonius; and more recently, in 51 B.C., he had re-visited Greece for further study. Thus he was well prepared to transmit Greek philosophy to his fellow Romans—and to later ages, for much of what we know of Hellenistic philosophy we owe to Cicero's patriotic intermediary efforts.

On the questions raised in Cicero's prefatory remarks to Brutus, see Catherine Saunders, "The Nature of Rome's Early Appraisal of Greek Culture," Classical Philology XXXIX (1944), 209-217, A convenient general work on Rome through the time of Cicero is F. R. Cowell, Cicero and the Roman Republic (Pelican Book).

From The Academic Questions, Treatise de Finibus, and Tusculan Disputations, trans. C. D. Yonge (London: Bohn, 1853).

GREEKS AND ROMANS
(*Tusculan Disputations* I, 1-6)

AT A TIME when I had entirely, or to a great degree, released myself from my labors as an advocate, and from my duties as a senator, I had recourse again, Brutus, principally by your advice, to those studies which never had been out of my mind, although neglected at times, and which after a long interval I resumed: and now since the principles and rules of all arts which relate to living well depend on the study of wisdom, which is called philosophy, I have thought it an employment worthy of me to illustrate them in the Latin tongue: not because philosophy could not be understood in the Greek language, or by the teaching of Greek masters; but it has always been my opinion, that our countrymen have, in some instances, made wiser discoveries than the Greeks, with reference to those subjects which they have considered worthy of devoting their attention to, and in others improved upon their discoveries, so that in one way or other we surpass them on every point: for, with regard to the manners and habits of private life, and family and domestic affairs, we certainly manage them with more elegance, and better than they did; and as to our republic, that our ancestors have, beyond all dispute, formed on better customs and laws. What shall I say of our military affairs; in which our ancestors have been most eminent in valor, and still more so in discipline? As to those things which are attained not by study, but nature, neither Greece, nor any nation, is comparable to us; for what people has displayed such gravity, such steadiness, such greatness of soul, probity, faith—such distinguished virtue of every kind, as to be equal to our ancestors. In learning indeed, and all kinds of literature, Greece did excel

us, and it was easy to do so where there was no competition; for
while amongst the Greeks the poets were the most ancient
species of learned men,—since Homer and Hesiod lived before
the foundation of Rome, and Archilochus was a contemporary
of Romulus,—we received poetry much later. For it was about
five hundred and ten years after the building of Rome before
Livius published a play in the consulship of C. Claudius, the
son of Caecus, and M. Tuditanus, a year before the birth of
Ennius, who was older than Plautus and Naevius.[1]

It was, therefore, late before poets were either known or received amongst us; though we find in Cato de Originibus[2] that
the guests used, at their entertainments, to sing the praises of
famous men to the sound of the flute; but a speech of Cato's
shows this kind of poetry to have been in no great esteem, as he
censures Marcus Nobilior, for carrying poets with him into his
province: for that consul, as we know, carried Ennius with him
into Aetolia. Therefore the less esteem poets were in, the less
were those studies pursued: though even then those who did
display the greatest abilities that way, were not very inferior to
the Greeks. Do we imagine that if it had been considered com-
mendable in Fabius, a man of the highest rank, to paint, we
should not have had many Polycleti and Parrhasii?[3] Honor
nourishes art, and glory is the spur with all to studies; while
those studies are always neglected in every nation, which are
looked upon disparagingly. The Greeks held skill in vocal and
instrumental music as a very important accomplishment, and
therefore it is recorded of Epaminondas, who, in my opinion,
was the greatest man amongst the Greeks, that he played excel-
lently on the flute; and Themistocles some years before was
deemed ignorant because at an entertainment he declined the
lyre when it was offered to him. For this reason musicians
flourished in Greece; music was a general study; and whoever
was unacquainted with it, was not considered as fully instructed
in learning. Geometry was in high esteem with them, therefore

none were more honorable than mathematicians; but we have confined this art to bare measuring and calculating.

But on the contrary, we early entertained an esteem for the orator; though he was not at first a man of learning, but only quick at speaking; in subsequent times he became learned; for it is reported that Galba, Africanus, and Laelius, were men of learning; and that even Cato, who preceded them in point of time, was a studious man: than succeeded the Lepidi, Carbo, and Gracchi, and so many great orators after them, down to our own times, that we were very little, if at all, inferior to the Greeks. Philosophy has been at a low ebb even to this present time, and has had no assistance from our own language, and so now I have undertaken to raise and illustrate it, in order that, as I have been of service to my countrymen, when employed on public affairs, I may, if possible, be so likewise in my retirement; and in this I must take the more pains, because there are already many books in the Latin language which are said to be written inaccurately, having been composed by excellent men, only not of sufficient learning: for indeed it is possible that a man may think well, and yet not be able to express his thoughts elegantly; but for any one to publish thoughts which he can neither arrange skilfully nor illustrate so as to entertain his reader, is an unpardonable abuse of letters and retirement: they, therefore, read their books to one another, and no one ever takes them up but those who wish to have the same licence for careless writing allowed to themselves. Wherefore, if oratory has acquired any reputation from my industry, I shall take the more pains to open the fountains of philosophy, from which all my eloquence has taken its rise.

---

[1] In 240 B.C. Livius Andronicus composed the first Latin comedy and the first Latin tragedy, both based on Greek models. His translation of the Odyssey, in the native Latin saturnian meter, was long standard as a school book.

2 Only fragments survive of the *Origines,* an historical work by M. Porcius Cato, the Censor (234-149 B.C.).
3 Fabius Pictor (whose grandson was the earliest Roman historian) painted murals on the temple of Salus in 302 B.C. Polyclitus was a famous Greek sculptor, Parrhasius a painter.

THE INFLUENCE OF PYTHAGORAS
(*Tusculan Disputations* IV, 1-7)

I HAVE often wondered, Brutus, on many occasions, at the ingenuity and virtues of our countrymen; but nothing has surprised me more than their development in those studies, which, though they came somewhat late to us, have been transported into this city from Greece. For the system of auspices, and religious ceremonies, the establishment of an army of cavalry and infantry, and the whole military discipline, were instituted as early as the foundation of the city by royal authority, partly too by laws, not without the assistance of the Gods. Then with what a surprising and incredible progress did our ancestors advance towards all kind of excellence, when once the republic was freed from the regal power! Not that this is a proper occasion to treat of the manners and customs of our ancestors, or of the discipline and constitution of the city; for I have elsewhere, particularly in the six books I wrote on the Republic, given a sufficiently accurate account of them. But whilst I am on this subject, and considering the study of philosophy, I meet with many reasons to imagine that those studies were brought to us from abroad, and not merely imported, but preserved and improved; for they had Pythagoras, a man of consummate wisdom and nobleness of character, in a manner, before their eyes; who was in Italy at the time that Lucius Brutus, the illustrious founder of your nobility, delivered his country from tyranny.[1]

As the doctrine of Pythagoras spread itself on all sides, it seems probable to me, that it reached this city; and this is not only probable of itself, but it does really appear to have been the case from many remains of it. For who can imagine that, when it flourished so much in that part of Italy which was called Magna Graecia, and in some of the largest and most powerful cities, in which, first the name of Pythagoras, and then that of those men who were afterwards his followers, was in so high esteem; who can imagine, I say, that our people could shut their ears to what was said by such learned men? Besides, it is even my opinion, that it was the great esteem in which the Pythagoreans were held, that gave rise to that opinion amongst those who came after him, that king Numa was a Pythagorean.[2] For, being acquainted with the doctrine and principles of Pythagoras, and having heard from their ancestors that this king was a very wise and just man, and not being able to distinguish accurately between times and periods that were so remote, they inferred from his being so eminent for his wisdom, that he had been a pupil of Pythagoras.

So far we proceed on conjecture. As to the vestiges of the Pythagoreans, though I might collect many, I shall use but a few; because they have no connexion with our present purpose. For, as it is reported to have been a custom with them to deliver certain precepts in a more abstruse manner in verse, and to bring their minds from severe thought to a more composed state by songs and musical instruments; so Cato, a writer of the very highest authority, says in his *Origins*, that it was customary with our ancestors for the guests at their entertainments, every one in his turn, to celebrate the praises and virtues of illustrious men in song to the sound of the flute; from whence it is clear that poems and songs were then composed for the voice. And, indeed, it is also clear that poetry was in fashion from the laws of the Twelve Tablets, wherein it is provided, that no song should be made to the injury of another. Another argument of the erudition of those times is, that they played on instruments before the shrines of their Gods, and at the entertainments of their magistrates; but that custom was peculiar to the sect I am speaking of. To me, indeed, that poem of Appius Caecus,[3] which Panaetius commends so much in a certain letter of his which is addressed to Quintus Tubero, has all the marks of a Pythagorean author. We have many things derived from the Pythagoreans in our customs; which I pass over, that we may not seem to have learned that elsewhere which we look upon ourselves as the inventors of. But to return to our purpose. How many great poets as well as orators have sprung up among us! and in what a short time! so that it is evident that our people could arrive at any learning as soon as they had an inclination for it. But of other studies I shall speak elsewhere if there is occasion, as I have already often done.

The study of philosophy is certainly of long standing with us; but yet I do not find that I can give you the names of any philosopher before the age of Laelius and Scipio: in whose younger days we find that Diogenes the Stoic, and Carneades the Academic, were sent as ambassadors by the Athenians to our senate.[4] And as these had never been concerned in public affairs, and one of them was a Cyrenean, the other a Babylonian, they certainly would never have been forced from their studies, nor chosen for that employment, unless the study of philosophy had been in vogue with some of the great men at that time; who, though they might employ their pens on other subjects, some on civil law, others on oratory, others on the history of former times, yet promoted this most extensive of all arts, the principle of living well, even more by their life than by their writings. So that of that true and elegant philosophy, (which was derived from Socrates, and is still preserved by the Peripatetics, and by the Stoics, though they express themselves differently in their disputes with the Academics) there are few or no Latin records; whether this proceeds from the importance of the thing itself, or from men's being otherwise employed, or from their concluding that the capacity of the people was not equal to the apprehension of them. But, during this silence, C. Amafinius[5] arose and took upon himself to speak; on the publishing of whose writings the people were moved, and enlisted themselves chiefly under this sect, either because the doctrine was more easily understood, or because they were invited thereto by the pleasing thoughts of amusement, or that, because there was nothing better, they laid hold of what was offered them. And after Amafinius, when many of the same sentiments had written much about them, the Pythagoreans spread over all Italy: but that these doctrines should be so easily understood and approved by the unlearned, it is a great proof that they were not written with any great subtlety, and they think their establishment to be owing to this. . . .

[1] By driving out Tarquinius Superbus, the last king of Rome (510 B.C.). Pythagoras had emigrated to Croton about twenty years earlier.

[2] Cf. Livy's critique of this notion (I, 18).

[3] As censor in 312 B.C. Appius Claudius Caecus built the Via Appia.

[4] In 156-155 B.C. fearing that they would exert a corrupting influence on the Romans, Cato had them dismissed.

[5] An older contemporary of Cicero, he popularized in Latin the philosophy of Epicurus, a philosophy which, for various reasons, found little favor in Cicero's eyes.

SALLUST

In Rome the writing of history had long been a proper activity of the governing class; and Sallust (86-35 B.C.) took pen in hand only after an active career as senator, tribune, praetor and governor of a province. His works date from what Ronald Syme has suggested we consider the "Triumviral Period," from Cicero's death down to the sixth consulate of Augustus in 28 B.C.—a brilliant fifteen years that also produced Horace's Epodes and Satires, Virgil's Eclogues and Georgics, Propertius' first book of elegies, and the earliest portion of Livy's history.

See Ronald Syme, Sallust (Berkeley & Los Angeles, 1964); Douglas Stewart, "Sallust and Fortuna," History and Theory VII (1968), 298-317; and, for a revisionist view of Sallust's subject, Arthur Kaplan, Catiline: the Man and his Role in the Roman Revolution (New York, 1968).

From Sallust, Florus, and Velleius Paterculus, trans. J. S. Watson (London: Bohn, 1852).

DECLINE IN MORALS
(*Catiline* V-XIII)

LUCIUS CATILINE was a man of noble birth, and of eminent mental and personal endowments; but of a vicious and depraved disposition. His delight, from his youth, had been in civil commotions, bloodshed, robbery, and sedition; and in such scenes he had spent his early years. His constitution could endure hunger, want of sleep, and cold, to a degree surpassing belief. His mind was daring, subtle, and versatile, capable of pretending or dissembling whatever he wished. He was covetous of other men's property, and prodigal of his own. He had abundance of eloquence, though but little wisdom. His insatiable ambition was always pursuing objects extravagant, romantic, and unattainable.

Since the time of Sulla's dictatorship, a strong desire of seizing the government possessed him, nor did he at all care, provided that he secured power for himself, by what means he might arrive at it. His violent spirit was daily more and more hurried on by the diminution of his patrimony, and by his consciousness of guilt; both which evils he had increased by those practices which I have mentioned above. The corrupt morals of the state, too, which extravagance and selfishness, pernicious and contending vices, rendered thoroughly depraved, furnished him with additional incentives to action.[1]

Since the occasion has thus brought public morals under my notice, the subject itself seems to call upon me to look back, and briefly to describe the conduct of our ancestors in peace and war; how they managed the state, and how powerful they left it; and how, by gradual alteration, it became, from being the most virtuous, the most vicious and depraved.

Of the city of Rome, as I understand, the founders and earliest inhabitants were the Trojans, who, under the conduct of Aeneas, were wandering about as exiles from their country, without any settled abode; and with these were joined the Aborigines, a savage race of men, without laws or government, free, and owning no control. How easily these two tribes, though of different origin, dissimilar language, and opposite ways of life, formed a union when they met within the same walls, is almost incredible. But when their state from an accession of population and territory, and an improved condition of morals, showed itself tolerably flourishing and powerful, envy, as is generally the case in human affairs, was the consequence of its prosperity. The neighboring kings and people, accordingly, began to assail them in war, while a few only of their friends came to their support; for the rest, struck with alarm, shrunk from sharing their dangers. But the Romans, active at home and in the field, prepared with alacrity for their defence. They encouraged one another, and hurried to meet the enemy. They protected, with their arms, their liberty, their country, and their homes. And when they had at length repelled danger by valor, they lent assistance to their allies and supporters, and procured friendships rather by bestowing favors than by receiving them.

They had a government regulated by laws. The denomination of their government was monarchy. Chosen men, whose bodies might be enfeebled by years, but whose minds were vigorous in understanding, formed the council of the state; and these, whether from their age, or from the similarity of their duty were called Fathers. But afterwards, when the monarchical power, which had been originally established for the protection of liberty, and for the promotion of the public interest, had degenerated into tyranny and oppression, they changed their plan, and appointed two magistrates, with power only annual; for they conceived that, by this method, the human mind would be least likely to grow overbearing through want of control.

At this period every citizen began to seek distinction, and to display his talents with greater freedom; for, with princes, the meritorious are greater objects of suspicion than the undeserving and to them the worth of others is a source of alarm. But when liberty was secured, it is almost incredible how much the state strengthened itself in a short space of time, so strong a passion for distinction had pervaded it. Now, for the first time, the youth, as soon as they were able to bear the toils of war, acquired military skill by actual service in the camp, and took pleasure rather in splendid arms and military steeds than in the society of mistresses and convivial indulgence. To such men no toil was unusual, no place was difficult or inaccessible, no armed enemy was formidable; their valor had overcome everything. But among themselves the grand rivalry was for glory; each sought to be first to wound an enemy, to scale a wall, and to be noticed while performing such an exploit. Distinction such as this they regarded as wealth, honor, and true nobility. They were covetous of praise, but liberal of money; they desired competent riches, but boundless glory. I could mention, but that the account would draw me too far from my subject, places in which the Roman people, with a small body of men, routed vast armies of the enemy; and cities which, though fortified by nature, they carried by assault.

But, assuredly, Fortune rules in all things. She makes everything famous or obscure rather from caprice than in conformity with truth. The exploits of the Athenians, as far as I can judge, were very great and glorious, yet something inferior to what fame has represented them. But because writers of great talent flourished there, the actions of the Athenians are celebrated over the world as the most splendid of achievements. Thus, the merit of those who have acted is estimated at the highest point to which illustrious intellects could exalt it in their writings.

But among the Romans there was never any such abundance

of writers; for with them, the most able men were the most actively employed. No one exercised the mind independently of the body; every man of ability chose to act rather than narrate, and was more desirous that his own merits should be celebrated by others, than that he himself should record theirs.

Good morals, accordingly, were cultivated in the city and in the camp. There was the greatest possible concord, and the least possible avarice. Justice and probity prevailed among the citizens, not more from the influence of the laws than from natural inclination. They displayed animosity, enmity, and resentment only against the enemy. Citizens contended with citizens in nothing but honor. They were magnificent in their religious services, frugal in their families, and steady in their friendships.

By those two virtues, intrepidity in war, and equity in peace, they maintained themselves and their state. Of their exercise of which virtues, I consider these as the greatest proofs: that, in war, punishment was oftener inflicted on those who attacked an enemy contrary to orders, and who, when commanded to retreat, retired too slowly from the contest, than on those who had dared to desert their standards, or, when pressed by the enemy, to abandon their posts; and that, in peace, they governed more by conferring benefits than by exciting terror, and, when they received an injury, chose rather to pardon than to revenge it.

But when, by perseverance and integrity, the republic had increased its power; when mighty princes had been vanquished in war; when barbarous tribes and populous states had been reduced to subjection; when Carthage, the rival of Rome's dominion, had been utterly destroyed, and sea and land lay everywhere open to her sway, Fortune then began to exercise her tyranny, and to introduce universal innovation. To those who had easily endured toils, dangers, and doubtful and difficult circumstances, ease and wealth, the objects of desire to others, became a burden and a trouble. At first the love of money, and then that of power, began to prevail, and these became, as it were, the sources of every evil. For avarice subverted honesty, integrity, and other honorable principles, and, in their stead, inculcated pride, inhumanity, contempt of religion, and general venality. Ambition prompted many to become deceitful; to keep one thing concealed in the breast, and another ready on the tongue; to estimate friendships and enmities, not by their worth, but according to interest; and to carry rather a specious countenance than an honest heart. These vices at first advanced but slowly, and were sometimes restrained by correction; but afterwards, when their infection had spread like a pestilence, the state was entirely changed, and the government, from being the most equitable and praiseworthy became rapacious and insupportable.

At first, however, it was ambition, rather than avarice, that influenced the minds of men; a vice which approaches nearer to virtue than the other. For of glory, honor, and power, the worthy is as desirous as the worthless; but the one pursues them by just methods; the other, being destitute of honorable qualities, works with fraud and deceit. But avarice has merely money for its object, which no wise man has ever immoderately desired. It is a vice which, as if imbued with deadly poison, enervates whatever is manly in body or mind. It is always unbounded and insatiable, and is abated neither by abundance nor by want.

But after Lucius Sulla, having recovered the government by force of arms,[2] proceeded, after a fair commencement, to a pernicious termination, all became robbers and plunderers; some set their affections on houses, others on lands; his victorious troops knew neither restraint nor moderation, but inflicted on the citizens disgraceful and inhuman outrages. Their rapacity was increased by the circumstance that Sulla, in order to secure the attachment of the forces which he had com-

manded in Asia, had treated them, contrary to the practice of
our ancestors, with extraordinary indulgence, and exemption
from discipline; and pleasant and luxurious quarters had easily,
during seasons of idleness, enervated the minds of the soldiery.
Then the armies of the Roman people first became habituated
to licentiousness and intemperance, and began to admire
statues, pictures, and sculptured vases; to seize such objects
alike in public edifices and private dwellings; to spoil temples;
and to cast off respect for everything, sacred and profane. Such
troops, accordingly, when once they obtained the mastery, left
nothing to the vanquished. Success unsettles the principles even
of the wise, and scarcely would those of debauched habits use
victory with moderation.

When wealth was once considered an honor, and glory,
authority, and power attended on it, virtue lost her influence,
poverty was thought a disgrace, and a life of innocence was regarded as a life of ill-nature. From the influence of riches, accordingly, luxury, avarice, and pride prevailed among the youth;
they grew at once rapacious and prodigal; they undervalued
what was their own, and coveted what was another's; they set at
nought modesty and continence; they lost all distinction between sacred and profane, and threw off all consideration and
self-restraint.

It furnishes much matter for reflection, after viewing our
modern mansions and villas extended to the size of cities, to
contemplate the temples which our ancestors, a most devout
race of men, erected to the Gods. But our forefathers adorned
the fanes of the deities with devotion, and their homes with
their own glory, and took nothing from those whom they conquered but the power of doing harm; their descendants, on the
contrary, the basest of mankind, have even wrested from their
allies, with the most flagrant injustice, whatever their brave
and victorious ancestors had left to their vanquished enemies;
as if the only use of power were to inflict injury.

For why should I mention those displays of extravagance, which can be believed by none but those who have seen them; as that mountains have been leveled, and seas covered with edifices, by many private citizens; men whom I consider to have made a sport of their wealth, since they were impatient to squander disreputably what they might have enjoyed with honor.

But the love of irregular gratification, open debauchery, and all kinds of luxury, had spread abroad with no less force. Men forgot their sex; women threw off all the restraints of modesty. To gratify appetite, they sought for every kind of production by land and sea; they slept before there was any inclination for sleep; they no longer waited to feel hunger, thirst, cold, or fatigue, but anticipated them all by luxurious indulgence. Such propensities drove the youth, when their patrimonies were exhausted, to criminal practices; for their minds, impregnated with evil habits, could not easily abstain from gratifying their passions, and were thus the more inordinately devoted in every way to rapacity and extravagance.

---

1 As consul in 63 B.C., Cicero thwarted Catiline's conspiracy.
2 Sulla returned from the East in 83 B.C. and became master of Italy the next year.

LIVY

A rhetorician and antiquarian rather than politician and man of action, Livy was in several senses the last of the republican writers. Recent scholarship has moved his date of birth from 59 back to 64 B.C.; and T. J. Luce has concluded that the first five books were completed by 27 B.C., and that "Instead of searching for Augustan allusions in Livian history, it might be more profitable to investigate to what extent Augustan policy was influenced by the Livian concept of the Roman past."

If Livy's "prose-epic is own sister to the Aeneid" (J. W. Duff), in its providential view of Roman history, they are not twin sisters, for Livy gazes resolutely backward to locate Rome's great age—in marked contrast to Virgil's eschatological interpretation of Rome's significance.

The standard book on Livy is now P. G. Walsh, Livy, His Historical Aims and Methods (Cambridge, 1961). On particular aspects of Livy's work, see Walsh, "Livy and Stoicism," American Journal of Philology LXXIX (1958), 355-75; T. J. Luce, "The Dating of Livy's First Decade," Transactions and Proceedings of the American Philological Association 96 (1965), 209-40; and John Pinsent, "Antiquarianism, Fiction and History in the First Decade of Livy," Classical Journal 55 (1959), 81-85.

ALEXANDER THE GREAT
VERSUS ROME
(*From the Founding of the City* IX, xvii-xix)

NOTHING can be thought to have been more remote from my intention, since I first set about this task, than to depart unduly from the order of events, and to aim, by the introduction of ornamental digressions, at providing as it were agreeable by-paths for the reader, and mental relaxation for myself. Nevertheless the mention of so great a prince and captain evokes certain thoughts which I have often silently pondered in my mind, and disposes me to enquire how the Roman State would have fared in a war with Alexander.

It appears that in war the factors of chief importance are the numbers and valor of the soldiers, the abilities of the commanders, and Fortune, which, powerful in all the affairs of men, is especially so in war. These factors, whether viewed separately or conjointly, afford a ready assurance, that, even as against other princes and nations, so also against this one the might of Rome would have proved invincible. First of all—to begin by comparing commanders—I do not deny that Alexander was a remarkable general; still, his fame was enhanced by the fact that he was a sole commander, and the further fact that he died young, in the flood-tide of success, when as yet he had experienced no other lot. Not to speak of other distinguished kings and generals, illustrious proofs of human vicissitude, what else was it but length of days that exposed Cyrus, whom the Greeks exalt so high in their panegyrics, to the fickleness of Fortune? And the same thing was lately seen in the case of Pompey the Great. Need I repeat the names of the Roman generals, not all nor of every age, but those very ones with whom, as consuls or

as dictators, Alexander would have had to fight—Marcus
Valerius Corvus, Gaius Marcius Rutulus, Gaius Sulpicius, Titus
Manlius Torquatus, Quintus Publilius Philo, Lucius Papirius
Cursor, Quintus Fabius Maximus, the two Decii, Lucius Volum-
nius, Manius Curius? After these come some extraordinary
men, if he had turned his attention to war with Carthage first
and later with Rome, and had crossed into Italy when somewhat old. Any one of these was highly endowed with courage
and talents as was Alexander; and military training, handed
down from the very beginning of the City, had taken on the
character of a profession, built up on comprehensive principles.
So the kings had warred; so after them the expellers of the kings,
the Junii and the Valerii, and so in succession the Fabii,
Quinctii, Cornelii, and Furius Camillus, whom in his old age
those had seen, as youths, who would have had to fight with
Alexander. But in the performance of a soldier's work in battle
—for which Alexander was no less distinguished—Manlius
Torquatus or Valerius Corvus would, forsooth, have yielded to
him, had they met him in hand-to-hand encounter, famous
though they were as soldiers before ever they won renown as
captains! The Decii, of course, would have yielded to him, who
hurled their devoted bodies upon the foe! Papirius Cursor
would have yielded, with that wondrous strength of body and
of spirit! The counsels of a single youth would no doubt have
got the better of that senate—not to speak of individual members—which was called an assembly of kings by him who before
all others had a true conception of the Roman Senate![1] And I
suppose there was the danger that Alexander would display
more skill than any of these whom I have named, in selecting
a place for a camp, in organizing his service of supply, in guarding against ambuscades, in choosing a time for battle, in marshal-
ling his troops, in providing strong reserves! He would have
said it was no Darius whom he had to deal with, trailing wom-
en and eunuchs after him, and weighed down with the gold

and purple trappings of his station.² Him he found a booty rather than an enemy, and conquered without bloodshed, merely by daring to despise vain shows. Far different from India, through which he progressed at the head of a rout of drunken revellers, would Italy have appeared to him, as he gazed on the passes of Apulia and the Lucanian mountains, and the still fresh traces of that family disaster wherein his uncle, King Alexander of Epirus, had lost his life.

And we are speaking of an Alexander not yet overwhelmed with prosperity, which none has ever been less able to bear. For viewing him in the light of his new fortune and of the new character—if I may use the expression—which he had assumed as conqueror, he would evidently have come to Italy more like Darius than like Alexander, at the head of an army that had forgotten Macedonia and was already adopting the degenerate customs of the Persians. I am loath, in writing of so great a prince, to remind the reader of the ostentatious alteration in his dress, and of his desire that men should prostrate themselves in adulation, a thing which even conquered Macedonians would have found oppressive, much more then those who had been victorious; of his cruel punishments and the murder of his friends as they drank and feasted; of the boastful lie about his origin.³ What if his love of wine had every day grown stronger? and his truculent and fiery anger? I mention only things which historians regard as certain. Can we deem such vices to be no detraction from a general's good qualities? But there was forsooth the danger—as the silliest of the Greeks,⁴ who exalt the reputation even of the Parthians against the Romans, are fond of alleging—that the Roman People would have been unable to withstand the majesty of Alexander's name, though I think that they had not so much as heard of him; and that out of all the Roman nobles not one would have dared to lift up his voice against him, although in Athens, a city crushed by the arms of Macedonia, at the very moment when men had before their eyes the reeking ruins of the neighboring Thebes, they dared inveigh against him freely, as witness the records of their speeches.

However imposing the greatness of the man may appear to us, still this greatness will be that of one man only, and the fruits of little more than ten years of success. Those who magnify it for this reason, that the Roman People, albeit never in any war, have yet suffered defeat in a number of battles,[5] whereas Alexander's fortune was never aught but prosperous in any battle, fail to perceive that they are comparing the achievements of a man—and a young man too—with those of a people that was now in its four hundredth year of warfare. Should it occasion us surprise if, seeing that upon the one side are counted more generations than are years upon the other, fortune should have varied more in that long time than in a life of thirteen years?[6] Why not compare a man's fortune with a man's, and a general's with a general's? How many Roman generals could I name who never suffered a reverse in battle! In our annals and lists of magistrates you may run through pages of consuls and dictators of whom it never on any day repented the Roman People, whether of their generalship or fortune. And what makes them more wonderful than Alexander or any king is this: some were dictators of ten or twenty days, and none held the consulship above a year; their levies were obstructed by the tribunes of the plebs; they were late in going to war, and were called back early to conduct elections; in the midst of their undertakings the year rolled round; now the rashness, now the forwardness of a colleague occasioned them losses or difficulties; they succeeded to affairs which others had mismanaged, they received an army of raw recruits, or one badly disciplined. Now consider kings: not only are they free from all impediments, but they are lords of time and circumstance, and in their counsels carry all things with them, instead of following in their train. So then, an undefeated Alexander would have warred against undefeated generals, and would have brought the same pledges of Fortune to the crisis. Nay, he would have run a greater risk than they, inasmuch as the Macedonians would have had but a single Alexander, not only exposed to many dangers, but incurring them voluntarily, while there would have been many Romans a match for Alexander, whether for glory or for the greatness of their deeds, of whom each several one would have lived and died as his own fate commanded, without endangering the State.

It remains to compare the forces on both sides, whether for numbers, or types of soldiers, or size of their contingents of auxiliaries. The quinquennial enumerations of that period put the population at 250,000. And so at the time when all the Latin allies were in revolt it was the custom to enroll ten legions, by a levy which was virtually limited to the City. In those years frequently four and five armies at a time would take the field, in Etruria, in Umbria (where they also fought the Gauls), in Samnium, and in Lucania. Later on Alexander would have found all Latium, with the Sabines, the Volsci and the Aequi, all Campania, and a portion of Umbria and Etruria, the Picentes and the Marsi and Paeligni, the Vestini and the Apulians, together with the whole coast of the Lower Sea, held by the Greeks, from Thurii as far as Naples and Cumae, and thence all the way to Antium and Ostia—all these, I say, he would have found either powerful friends of the Romans or their defeated enemies. He himself would have crossed the sea with veteran Macedonians to the number of not more than thirty thousand foot and four thousand horse—mostly Thessalians—for this was his main strength. If to these he had added Persians and Indians and other nations, he would have found them a greater burden to have dragged about than a help.

Add to this, that the Romans would have had recruits ready to call upon, but Alexander, as happened afterwards to Hannibal, would have found his army wear away, while he warred

in a foreign land. His men would have been armed with tar-
gets and spears: the Romans with an oblong shield, affording
more protection to the body, and the Roman javelin, which
strikes, on being thrown, with a much harder impact than the
lance. Both armies were formed of heavy troops, keeping to
their ranks; but their phalanx was immobile and consisted of
soldiers of a single type; the Roman line was opener and com-
prised more separate units; it was easy to divide, wherever
necessary, and easy to unite. Moreover, what soldier can
match the Roman in entrenching? Who is better at enduring
toil? Alexander would, if beaten in a single battle, have been
beaten in the war; but what battle could have overthrown the
Romans, whom Caudium could not overthrow, nor Cannae?
Nay, many a time—however prosperous the outset of his enterprise might have been—would he have wished for Indians and
Persians and unwarlike Asiatics, and would have owned that he
had before made war upon women, as Alexander, King of
Epirus, is reported to have said, when mortally wounded, in
contrasting the type of war waged by this very youth in Asia,
with that which had fallen to his own share.[7]

Indeed when I remember that we contended against the
Carthaginians on the seas for four-and-twenty years, I think
that the whole life of Alexander would hardly have sufficed for
this single war; and perchance, inasmuch as the Punic State
had been by ancient treaties leagued with the Romans, and
the two cities most powerful in men and arms might well have
made common cause against the foe whom both dreaded, he
had been crushed beneath the simultaneous attacks of Rome
and Carthage. The Romans have been at war with the Macedonians—not, to be sure, when Alexander led them or their
prosperity was unimpaired, but against Antiochus, Philippus,
and Perses—and not only without ever suffering defeat, but
even without incurring any danger. Proud word I would not
speak, but never—and may civil wars be silent!—never have we

been beaten by infantry, never in open battle, never on even, or at all events on favorable ground: cavalry and arrows, impassable defiles, regions that afford no road to convoys, may well occasion fear in heavy-armed troops.[8] A thousand battle-arrays more formidable than those of Alexander and the Macedonians have the Romans beaten off—and shall do—if only our present love of domestic peace endure and our concern to maintain concord.

[1] Cineas, a Thessalian diplomat employed by King Pyrrhus of Epirus (who defeated the Romans in 280 and 279 B.C. but failed to establish himself in Italy).

[2] Darius III, whom Alexander defeated in the battle of Arbela (331 B.C.).

[3] The claim that Zeus, not Philip, was his father.

[4] On the probable identity of Rome's critic, and on the other questions posed by Livy's excursus, see Luce, 218-229.

[5] Cf. Lucilius (Marx: 613-614): "The Roman people have been overcome by force and conquered in many battles, but never in a war—which is what really counts."

[6] That is, Alexander's reign from 336 to 323 B.C.

[7] Cf. Aulus Gellius, Noctes Atticae XVII, xxi, 33.

[8] Livy has painfully in mind the Parthian cavalry and archers, who had defeated Crassus in the desert (53 B.C.) and had also harassed Antony in the mountains. This passage presumably dates, then, from before the recovery of Crassus' lost standards (20 B.C.), which was a highly lauded accomplishment.

THEODOR MOMMSEN

The three volumes of Mommsen's History of Rome (through the time of Caesar) which appeared in 1854-56 immediately established him as the leading authority on the Republic; and his enduring literary merits were officially recognized by the award of a Nobel Prize almost forty years later. Though details of his history have of course been outdated by subsequent research (much of it facilitated by his own edition of the Corpus Inscriptionum Latinarum), his work, like Gibbon's, retains a quality of permanence shared by hardly any others written by their contemporaries. History's greatest subject has felicitiously inspired the two greatest classics of modern historiography.

There is a fine appreciation of Mommsen as a man and as an historian in the abridgement edited by Dero A. Saunders and John A. Collins (Meridian Books, 1958). On various forms of opposition to, and deviation from, the system Caesar established, see Ramsay MacMullen, Enemies of the Roman Order: Treason, Unrest, and Alienation in the Empire (Cambridge, Mass., 1966).

From The History of Rome, trans. W. P. Dickson, volume V (New York: Scribner's, 1895).

CAESAR'S ACHIEVEMENT
(*The History of Rome* V, xi)

. . . THE republican opposition submitted to be pardoned; but it was not reconciled. Discontent with the new order of things and exasperation against the unwonted ruler were general. For open political resistance there was indeed no farther opportunity—it was hardly worth taking into account, that some oppositional tribunes on occasion of the question of title acquired for themselves the republican crown of martyrdom by a demonstrative intervention against those who had called Caesar king—but republicanism found expression all the more decidedly as an opposition of sentiment, and in secret agitation and plotting. Not a hand stirred when the Imperator appeared in public. There was abundance of wall-placards and sarcastic verses full of bitter and telling popular satire against the new monarchy. When a comedian ventured on a republican allusion, he was saluted with the loudest applause. The praise of Cato formed the fashionable theme of oppositional pamphleteers, and their writings found a public all the more grateful because even literature was no longer free. Caesar indeed combated the republicans even now on their own field; he himself and his abler confidants replied to the Cato-literature with Anticatones, and the republican and Caesarian scribes fought round the dead hero of Utica like the Trojans and Hellenes round the dead body of Patroclus; but as a matter of course in this conflict—where the public thoroughly republican in its feelings was judge—the Caesarians had the worst of it. No course remained but to overawe the authors; on which account men well known and dangerous in a literary point of view, such as Publius Nigidius Figulus and Aulus Caecina, had more difficulty in obtaining permission to return to Italy than other exiles, while the oppositional writers tolerated in Italy were subjected to a practical censorship, the restraints of which were all the more annoying that the measure of punishment to be dreaded was utterly arbitrary. The underground machinations of the overthrown parties against the new monarchy will be more fitly set forth in another connection. Here it is sufficient to say that risings of pretenders as well as of republicans were incessantly brewing throughout the Roman empire; that the flames of civil war kindled now by the Pompeians, now by the republicans, again burst forth brightly at various places; and that in the capital there was perpetual conspiracy against the life of the monarch. But Caesar could not be induced by these plots even to surround himself permanently with a body-guard, and usually contented himself with making known the detected conspiracies by public placards.

However much Caesar was wont to treat all things relating to his personal safety with daring indifference, he could not possibly conceal from himself the very serious danger with which this mass of malcontents threatened not merely himself but also his creations. If nevertheless, disregarding all the warning and urgency of his friends, he without deluding himself as to the implacability of the very opponents to whom he showed mercy, persevered with marvellous composure and energy in the course of pardoning by far the greater number of them, he did so neither from the chivalrous magnanimity of a proud, nor from the sentimental clemency of an effeminate, nature, but from the correct statesmanly consideration that vanquished parties are disposed of more rapidly and with less public injury by their absorption within the state than by any attempt to extirpate them by proscription or to eject them from the commonwealth by banishment. Caesar could not for his high objects dispense with the constitutional party itself, which in fact embraced not the aristocracy merely but all the

elements of a free and national spirit among the Italian bur-
gesses; for his schemes, which contemplated the renovation of
the antiquated state, he needed the whole mass of talent, culture, hereditary and self-acquired distinction, which this party
embraced; and in this sense he may well have named the pardoning of his opponents the finest reward of victory. Accordingly the most prominent chiefs of the defeated parties were
indeed removed, but full pardon was not withheld from the
men of the second and third rank and especially of the younger generation; they were not, however, allowed to sulk in pas-
sive opposition, but were by more or less gentle pressure induced to take an active part in the new administration, and to
accept honors and offices from it. As with Henry the Fourth,
and William of Orange, so with Caesar his greatest difficulties
began only after the victory. Every revolutionary conqueror
learns by experience that, if after vanquishing his opponents
he would not remain like Cinna and Sulla, a mere party-chief,
but would like Caesar, Henry the Fourth, and William of
Orange substitute the welfare of the commonwealth for the
necessarily one-sided program of his own party, for the moment all parties, his own as well as the vanquished, unite against
the new chief; and the more so, the more great and pure his
idea of his new vocation. The friends of the constitution and
the Pompeians, though doing homage with the lips to Caesar,
bore yet in heart a grudge either at monarchy or at least at the
dynasty; the degenerate democracy was in open rebellion
against Caesar from the moment of its perceiving that Caesar's
objects were by no means its own; even the personal adherents
of Caesar murmured, when they found that their chief was
establishing instead of a state of *condottieri* a monarchy equal
and just towards all, and that the portions of gain accruing to
them were to be diminished by the accession of the vanquished. This settlement of the commonwealth was acceptable
to no party, and had to be imposed on his associates no less

than on his opponents. Caesar's own position was now in a certain sense more imperilled than before the victory; but what he lost, the state gained. By annihilating the parties and not simply sparing the partisans but allowing every man of talent or even merely of good descent to attain to office irrespective of his political past, he gained for his great building all the working power extant in the state; and not only so, but the voluntary or compulsory participation of men of all parties in the same work led the nation also over imperceptibly to the newly prepared ground. The fact that this reconciliation of the parties was for the moment only external and that they were for the present much less agreed in adherence to the new state of things than in hatred against Caesar, did not mislead him; he knew well that antagonisms lose their keenness when brought into such outward union; and that only in this way can the statesman anticipate the work of time, which alone is able finally to heal such a strife by laying the old generation in the grave. Still less did he inquire who hated him or meditated his assassination. Like every genuine statesman he served not the people for reward—not even for the reward of their love—but sacrificed the favor of his contemporaries for the blessing of posterity, and above all for the permission to save and renew his nation.

In attempting to give a detailed account of the mode in which the transition was effected from the old to the new state of things, we must first of all recollect that Caesar came not to begin, but to complete. The plan of a new policy suited to the times, long ago projected by Gaius Gracchus, had been maintained by his adherents and successors with more or less of spirit and success, but without wavering. Caesar, from the outset and as it were by hereditary right the head of the popular party, had for thirty years borne aloft its banner without ever changing or even so much as concealing his colors; he remained democrat even when monarch. As he accepted without limitation, apart of course from the preposterous projects of Catilina and Clodius, the heritage of his party; as he displayed the bitterest, even personal, hatred to the aristocracy and the genuine aristocrats; and as he retained unchanged the essential ideas of Roman democracy, viz. alleviation of the burden of debtors, transmarine colonization, gradual equalization of the differences of rights among the classes belonging to the state, emancipation of the executive power from the senate: his monarchy was so little at variance with democracy, that democracy on the contrary only attained its completion and fulfilment by means of that monarchy. For this monarchy was not the Oriental despotism of divine right, but a monarchy such as Gaius Gracchus wished to found, such as Pericles and Cromwell founded—the representation of the nation by the man in whom it puts supreme and unlimited confidence. The ideas, which lay at the foundation of Caesar's work, were so far not strictly new; but to him belongs their realization, which after all is everywhere the main matter; and to him pertains the grandeur of execution, which would probably have surprised the brilliant projector himself if he could have seen it, and which has impressed, and will always impress, every one to whom it has been presented in the living reality or in the mirror of history—to whatever historical epoch or whatever shade of politics he may belong—according to the measure of his ability to comprehend human and historical greatness, with deep and ever-deepening emotion and admiration.

At this point however it is proper expressly once for all to claim what the historian everywhere tacitly presumes, and to protest against the custom—common to simplicity and perfidy —of using historical praise and historical censure, dissociated from the given circumstances, as phrases of general application, and in the present case of construing the judgment as to Caesar into a judgment as to what is called Caesarism. It is true that the history of past centuries ought to be the instructress of the present; but not in the vulgar sense, as if one could simply by turning over the leaves discover the conjunctures of the present in the records of the past, and collect from these the symptoms for a political diagnosis and the specifics for a prescription; it is instructive only so far as the observation of older forms of culture reveals the organic conditions of civilization generally —the fundamental forces everywhere alike, and the manner of their combination everywhere different—and leads and encourages men, not to unreflecting imitation, but to independent reproduction. In this sense the history of Caesar and of Roman Imperialism, with all the unsurpassed greatness of the master-worker, is in truth a sharper censure of modern autocracy than could be written by the hand of man. According to the same law of nature in virtue of which the smallest organism infinitely surpasses the most artistic machine, every constitution however defective which gives play to the free self-determination of a majority of citizens infinitely surpasses the most brilliant and humane absolutism; for the former is capable of development and therefore living, the latter is what it is and therefore dead. This law of nature has verified itself all the more completely, that, under the impulse of its creator's genius and in the absence of all material complications from without, that monarchy developed itself more purely and freely than any similar state. From Caesar's time, as the sequel will show and Gibbon has shown long ago, the Roman system had only an external coherence and received only a mechanical extension, while internally it became even with him utterly withered and dead. If in the early stages of the autocracy and above all in Caesar's own soul the hopeful dream of a combination of free popular development and absolute power was still cherished, the government of the highly-gifted emperors of the Julian house soon taught men in a terrible form how far it was possible to hold fire and water in the same vessel. Caesar's work was necessary and salutary, not because it was or could be fraught with blessings in itself, but because—with the national organization of antiquity, which was based on slavery and was utterly a stranger to republican-constitutional representation, and in presence of the legitimate urban constitution which in the course of five hundred years had ripened into oligarchic absolutism—absolute military monarchy was the copestone logically necessary and the least of evils. When once the slave-holding aristocracy in Virginia and the Carolinas shall have carried matters as far as their congeners in the Sullan Rome, Caesarism will there too be legitimized at the bar of the spirit of history;[1] where it appears under other conditions of development, it is at once a caricature and a usurpation. But history will not submit to curtail the true Caesar of his due honor, because her verdict may in the presence of bad Caesars lead simplicity astray and may give to roguery occasion for lying and fraud. She too is a Bible, and if she cannot any more than the Bible hinder the fool from misunderstanding and the devil from quoting her, she too will be able to bear with, and to requite, them both. . . .

Such were the foundations of the Mediterranean monarchy of Caesar. For the second time in Rome the social question had reached a crisis, at which the antagonisms not only appeared to be, but actually were, in the form of their exhibition, insoluble and, in the form of their expression, irreconcilable. On the former occasion Rome had been saved by the fact that Italy was merged in Rome and Rome in Italy, and in the new enlarged and altered home those old antagonisms were not reconciled, but fell into abeyance. Now Rome was once more saved by the fact that the countries of the Mediterranean were merged in it or became prepared for merging; the war between the Italian poor and rich, which in the old Italy could only end with the destruction of the nation, had no longer a battlefield or a meaning in the Italy of three continents. The Latin

colonies closed the gap which threatened to swallow up the
Roman community in the fifth century; the deeper chasm of
the seventh century was filled by the Transalpine and transmarine colonizations of Gaius Gracchus and Caesar. For Rome
alone history not merely performed miracles, but also repeated
its miracles, and twice cured the internal crisis, which in the
state itself was incurable, by regenerating the state. There was
doubtless much corruption in this regeneration; as the union
of Italy was accomplished over the ruins of the Samnite and
Etruscan nations, so the Mediterranean monarchy built itself
on the ruins of countless states and tribes once living and vigorous; but it was a corruption out of which sprang a fresh
growth, part of which remains green at the present day. What
was pulled down for the sake of the new building, was merely
the secondary nationalities which had long since been marked
out for destruction by the leveling hand of civilization. Caesar,
wherever he came forward as a destroyer, only carried out the
pronounced verdict of historical development; but he protected
the germs of culture, where and as he found them, in his own
land as well as among the sister nation of the Hellenes. He
saved and renewed the Roman type; and not only did he spare
the Greek type, but with the renewed foundation of Rome he
undertook also the regeneration of the Hellenes, and resumed
the interrupted work of the great Alexander, whose image, we
may well believe, never was absent from Caesar's soul. He
solved these two great tasks not merely side by side, but the
one by means of the other. The two great essentials of humanity—general and individual development, or state and culture—
once in embryo united in those old Graeco-Italians feeding
their flocks in primeval simplicity far from the coasts and islands of the Mediterranean, had become dissevered when these
were parted into Italians and Hellenes, and had thenceforth
remained apart for many centuries. Now the descendant of the

Trojan prince and the Latin king's daughter created out of a state without distinctive culture and a cosmopolitan civilization a new whole, in which state and culture again met together at the acme of human existence in the rich fulness of blessed maturity and worthily filled the sphere appropriate to such an union.

The outlines have thus been set forth, which Caesar drew for this work, according to which he labored himself, and according to which posterity—for many centuries confined to the paths which this great man marked out—endeavored to prosecute the work, if not with the intellect and energy, yet on the whole in accordance with the intentions, of the illustrious master. Little was finished; much even was merely begun. Whether the plan was complete, those who venture to vie in thought with such a man may decide; we observe no material defect in what lies before us—every single stone of the building enough to make a man immortal, and yet all combining to form one harmonious whole. Caesar ruled as king of Rome for five years and a half, not half as long as Alexander; in the intervals of seven great campaigns, which allowed him to stay not more than fifteen months altogether in the capital of his empire, he regulated the destinies of the world for the present and the future, from the establishment of the boundary-line between civilization and barbarism down to the removal of the pools of rain in the streets of the capital, and yet retained time and composure enough attentively to follow the prize-pieces in the theatre and to confer the chaplet on the victor with improvised verses. The rapidity and self-precision with which the plan was executed prove that it had been long meditated thoroughly and all its parts settled in detail; but, even thus, they remain not much less wonderful than the plan itself. The outlines were laid down and thereby the new state was defined for all coming time; the boundless future alone could complete the structure. So far Caesar might say, that his aim was attained; and this was probably the meaning of the words which were sometimes heard to fall from him— that he had "lived enough." But precisely because the building was an endless one, the master as long as he lived restlessly added stone to stone, with always the same dexterity and always the same elasticity busy at his work, without ever over- turning or postponing, just as if there were for him merely a to-day and no to-morrow. Thus he worked and created as never did any mortal before or after him; and as a worker and creator he still, after wellnigh two thousand years, lives in the memory of the nations—the first, and withal unique, Imperator Caesar.

(Conclusion: V, xii)

. . . We have reached the end of the Roman republic. We have seen it rule for five hundred years in Italy and in the coun- tries on the Mediterranean; we have seen it brought to ruin in politics and morals, religion and literature, not through out- ward violence but through inward decay, and thereby making room for the new monarchy of Caesar. There was in the world, as Caesar found it, much of the noble heritage of past centuries and an infinite abundance of pomp and glory, but little spirit, still less taste, and least of all true delight in life. It was indeed an old world; and even the richly-gifted patriotism of Caesar could not make it young again. The dawn does not return till after the night has fully set in and run its course. But yet with him there came to the sorely harassed peoples on the Mediter- ranean a tolerable evening after the sultry noon; and when at length after a long historical night the new day dawned once more for the peoples, and fresh nations in free self-movement commenced their race towards new and higher goals, there were found among them not a few, in which the seed sown by Caesar had sprung up, and which owed, as they still owe, to him their national individuality.

1 Mommsen later added this note: "When this was written—in the year 1857 —no one could foresee how soon the mightiest struggle and most glorious victory as yet recorded in human annals would save the United States from this fearful trial, and secure the future existence of an absolute self-governing freedom not to be permanently kept in check by any local Caesarism."

PART TWO: IMPERIAL ROME

I haste to tell thee, nor shall Shame oppose,
What Confidents our Wealthy *Romans* chose:
And whom I most abhor: To speak my Mind,
I hate, in *Rome*, a *Grecian* Town to find:
To see the Scum of *Greece* transplanted here,
Receiv'd like Gods, is what I cannot bear.
Nor *Greeks* alone, but *Syrians* here abound,
Obscene *Orontes*, diving under Ground,
Conveys his Wealth to *Tyber's* hungry Shoars,
And fattens *Italy* with Foreign Whores:
Hither their crooked Harps and Customs come;
All find Receipt in Hospitable *Rome*.

Juvenal, *Satire* III, 58-65 (trans. Dryden)

VIRGIL

In contrast to other classical writers, Virgil had a teleological view
of history as divinely ordered process—a view quite comparable
with the Hebraic, and later the Augustinian, eschatological interpretation of history. Rome had a mission, to establish universal
peace; and all previous history leads to the Augustan Principate.
In Brooks Otis' words, "his epic is the unique history of his own
unique people, or rather the fateful beginning of that history.
There has been nothing like it. It is decisive precisely because it
breaks the old patterns and makes another better than them all"
(p. 60). But while it celebrates Rome's achievements, the Aeneid
also illustrates their horrible cost, to both victor and vanquished:
the best commentary on the poem may ultimately be Freud's Civilization and its Discontents.

See Chester Starr, "Virgil's Acceptance of Octavian," American
Journal of Philology LXXVI (1955), 34-46; Brooks Otis, "Virgil
and Cleo: A Consideration of Virgil's Relation to History," Phoenix XX (1966), 59-75; and David Thompson, "Allegory and Typol-
ogy in the Aeneid," Arethusa 3 (Fall, 1970), 147-153.

Pitt's translation is reprinted (in slightly adapted form) from The
Works of the English Poets, volume XIX (London, 1810).

RULE WITHOUT END
(*Aeneid* I, 257-296)

"Daughter, dismiss your fears; by doom divine
Fixed are the fates of your immortal line.[1]
Your eyes Lavinium's promised walls shall see,
And here we ratify our first decree.
Your son, the brave Aeneas, soon shall rise,
Himself a god, and mount the starry skies.
To soothe your care, these secrets I relate
From the dark volumes of eternal fate:
The chief fair Italy shall reach, and there
With mighty nations wage a dreadful war,
New cities raise, the savage nations awe,
And to the conquered kingdoms give the law.
The fierce Rutulians vanquished by his sword,
Three years shall Latium own him sovereign lord.
Your dear Ascanius then, the royal boy,
(Now called Iülus, since the fall of Troy)
While thirty rolling years their orbs complete,
Shall wear the crown, and from Lavinium's seat
Transfer the kingdom; and, of mighty length
Raise towering Alba, glorying in her strength.
There shall the Trojan race enjoy the power,
And fill the throne three hundred winters more.
Ilia, the royal priestess, next shall bear
Two lovely infants to the god of war.
Nursed by a tawny wolf, her eldest son,
Imperial Romulus, shall mount the throne;
From his own name, the people Romans call,
And from his father Mars, his rising wall.

No limits have I fixed, of time, or place,
To the vast empire of the godlike race.
Even haughty Juno shall the nations love,
Who now alarms earth, seas, and Heaven above;
And join her friendly counsels to my own,
With endless fame the sons of Rome to crown,
The world's majestic lords, the nation of the gown.
This word be fate—an hour shall wing its way,
When Troy in dust shall proud Mycenae lay.
In Greece, Assaracus' sons shall reign,[2]
And vanquished Argos wear the victor's chain.
Then Caesar, called by great Iülus' name,
(Whose empire ocean bounds, the stars his fame)
Sprung from the noble Trojan line, shall rise,
Charged with his eastern spoils, and mount the skies.
Him shall you see, advanced to these abodes—
Adored by Rome, a god among the gods.
From that blest hour all violence shall cease,
The age grow mild, and soften into peace.
With righteous Remus shall Quirinus reign,
Old faith, and Vesta, shall return again;
With many a solid hinge, and brazen bar,
Shall Janus close the horrid gates of war.[3]
Within the temple Fury shall be bound,
With a huge heap of shattered arms around;
Wrapped in a hundred chains, beneath the load
The fiend shall roar, and grind his teeth in blood."

---

[1] Jupiter is reassuring Venus, mother of Aeneas. On the fusing of the Aeneas and the Romulus legends, and on the actual archeological data, see John A. Brinkman, S.J., "The Foundation Legends in Vergil," *Classical Journal* 54 (1958), 25-33. Father Brinkman observes that "there were definitely no settlements at Rome in the twelfth century (when Aeneas was supposed to have arrived), and Rome was not made into one city until about a century and a half after the traditional date for Romulus, 753 B.C." (p. 32).

[2] Assaracus was the son of Tros, and grandfather of Aeneas' father, Anchises.
[3] On Numa's establishment of the temple of Janus, see Livy I, 19. When closed, it indicated that Rome was at peace with all surrounding nations; this had occurred at the conclusion of the second Punic war, then following the battle of Actium (31 B.C.) and after the subjection of Spain in 27-25 B.C.

ROME'S HISTORY AND MISSION
(*Aeneid* VI, 756-853)

"Now hear, while I display our race divine,[1]
And the long glories of our Dardan line,
The noble Roman heroes, who shall rise
From Trojan blood, in series, to the skies.
This mighty scene of wonder I relate,
And open all your glorious future fate.
First then behold yon blooming youth appear,
That hero leaning on his shining spear!
This your last son, your hoary age shall grace,
Your first brave offspring of the Latin race;
From fair Lavinia in the groves he springs,
A king, and father of a race of kings,
Sylvius his name. Proud Alba shall he sway,
And to his sons the imperial power convey.
See! where the youth, already winged to rise,
Stands on the verge of life, and claims the skies.
Procas the next behold, a chief divine,
Procas the glory of the Trojan line.
Capys and Numitor there pant for fame;
There a new Sylvius bears your mighty name:
Like you, just, great, and good, for valor known,
The chief shall mount the imperial Alban throne.

What strength each youth displays!" "But who are those
With civic crowns around their manly brows?"
"By those shall Gabii and Nomentum rise,
And proud Collatian towers invade the skies.
Then Faunus' town with turrets shall be crowned,
And fair Fidena stretch her ramparts round.
Then Bola too shall rise, of mighty fame;
Unpeopled now they lie, and lands without a name!
Bright Ilia, sprung from Trojan blood, shall bear
Yon glorious hero to the god of war:[2]
Behold great Romulus, her victor son,
Whose sword restores his grandsire to the throne.
Lo! from his helmet what a glory plays!
And Jove's own splendors round his temples blaze.
From this brave prince majestic Rome shall rise:
The boundless Earth, her empire shall comprise;
Her fame and valor tower above the skies!
Seven ample hills the imperial city grace,
Who nobly glories in her martial race;
Proud of her sons, she lifts her head on high;
Proud, as the mighty mother of the sky,[3]
When through the Phrygian towns, sublime in air,
She rides triumphant in her golden car,
Crowned with a nodding diadem of towers,
And counts her offspring, the celestial powers,
A shining train, who fill the blest abode,
A hundred sons, and every son a god!
Turn, turn your eyes! see here your race divine,
Behold your own imperial Roman line:
Caesar, with all the Julian name survey;
See where the glorious ranks ascend to day!
This—this is he!—the chief so long foretold
To bless the land where Saturn ruled of old,
And give the Lernean realms a second age of gold!

The promised prince, Augustus the divine,
Of Caesar's race, and Jove's immortal line!
This mighty chief his empire shall extend
O'er Indian realms, to Earth's remotest end.
The hero's rapid victories outrun
The year's whole course, the stars, and journeys of the Sun!
Where, high in air, huge Atlas' shoulders rise,
Support the ethereal lights, and prop the rolling skies!
He comes!—he comes!—proclaimed by every god!
Nile hears the shout, and shakes in every flood.
Proud Asia flies before his dire alarms,
And distant nations tremble at his arms.
So many realms not great Alcides past,
Not when the brazen-footed hind he chased;
O'er Erymanthus' steeps the boar pursued;
Or drew the huge Lernean monster's blood.
Nor Bacchus such a length of regions knew,
When on his car the god in triumph flew,
And shook the reins, and urged the fiery wheels,
Whirled by swift tigers down the Indian hills.
And doubt we yet, by virtuous deeds to rise,
When fame, when empire is the certain prize?
Rise, rise my son; your Latin foes o'ercome!
Rise, the great founder of majestic Rome!"
"But who that chief, who crowned with olive stands,
And holds the sacred relics in his hands?"
"I know the pious Roman king from far,[4]
The silver beard, and venerable hair;
Called from his little barren field away,
To pomp of empire and the regal sway.
Tullus the next succeeds, whose loud alarms
Shall rouse the slumbering sons of Rome to arms.
Inspired by him, the soft unwarlike train

Repeat their former triumphs o'er again.
Lo Ancus there! the giddy crowd he draws,
And swells too much with popular applause.
Now would you Tarquin's haughty race behold,
Or fierce avenging Brutus, brave and bold?
See the stern chief stalk awful o'er the plain,
The glorious chief, who breaks the tyrant's chain:
He to his axe shall proud rebellion doom,
The first great consul of his rescued Rome!
His sons (who arm, the Tarquins to maintain,
And fix oppression in the throne again)
He nobly yields to justice, in the cause
Of sacred freedom and insulted laws.
Though harsh the uphappy father may appear,
The judge compels the sire to be severe;
And the fair hopes of fame the patriot move,
To sink the private in the public love.
    "Like him, Torquatus, for stern justice known,
Dooms to the axe his brave victorious son.
Behold the Drusi prodigal of blood!
The Decii dying for their country's good!
Behold Camillus there; that chief shall come
With four proud triumphs to imperial Rome.
Lo! in bright arms two spirits rise to sight![5]
How close their friendship in the realms of night!
How fierce their discord when they spring to light!
How furious in the field will both appear!
With what dire slaughter! what a waste of war!
Impetuous to the fight the father pours
From the steep Alps, and tall Ligurian towers.
The son, with servile monarchs in his train,
Leads the whole Eastern world, and spreads the plain.
Oh! check your wrath, my sons; the nations spare;

And save your country from the woes of war;
Nor in her sacred breast, with rage abhorred,
So fiercely plunge her own victorious sword!
And you, be you the first: your arms resign,
You, my great son of Jove's celestial line!
     "Yon chief shall vanquish all the Grecian powers,
And lay in dust the proud Corinthian towers,
Drive to the capitol his gilded car,
And grace the triumph with the spoils of war.[6]
That chief shall stretch fair Argos on the plain,
And the proud seat of Agamemnon's reign,
O'ercome the Aeacian king, of race divine,
Sprung from the great Achilles' glorious line;[7]
Avenge Minerva's violated fane,
And the great spirits of your fathers slain.
What tongue, just Cato, can your praise forbear!
Or each brave Scipio's noble deeds declare,
Afric's dread foes; two thunderbolts of war!
Who can the bold Fabricius' worth repeat,
In pride of poverty, divinely great;
Called by his country's voice to come
From the rude plough, and rule imperial Rome![8]
Tired as I am the glorious roll to trace,
Where am I snatched by the long Fabian race!
See where the patriot shines, whose prudent care
Preserves his country by protracted war![9]
     "The subject nations, with a happier grace,
From the rude stone may call the mimic face,
Or with the new life inform the breathing brass;
Shine at the bar, describe the stars on high,
The motions, laws, and regions of the sky.
Be this your nobler praise in times to come,
These your imperial arts, you sons of Rome:
O'er distant realms to stretch your awful sway,

To bid those nations tremble and obey;
To crush the proud, the suppliant foe to rear,
To give mankind a peace, or shake the world with war."

1 Anchises' shade is showing Aeneas the souls of his Alban and Roman posterity.
2 On the following lines see Robert J. Getty, "Romulus, Roma, and Augustus
  in the Sixth Book of the *Aeneid*," *Classical Philology* XLV (1950), 1-12.
3 Cybele (whose worship came to Rome from Phrygia) was worshipped as
  Magna Mater, the mother of the gods.
4 The roll call of kings resumes with Numa Pompilius.
5 The antagonists in the Civil War, Julius Caesar and his son-in-law, Pompey.
6 L. Mummius had a famous triumph after conquering Greece and destroying
  Corinth in 146 B.C.
7 Macedon was conquered in 168 B.C. by L. Aemilius Paullus. Perseus, the defeated king, was supposedly a descendant of Achilles.
8 This portion of Pitt's translation is far from satisfactory. He has omitted Cossus
  (consul in 428 B.C.) and the Gracchi, reformers who were slain (133 and
  122 B.C.) for their championship of the people; and conflated what Virgil
  says about Fabricius (consul in 282 and 278 B.C. and famous for refusing
  bribes from Pyrrhus) and Serranus, who was called to the consulship from
  the plough in 257 B.C.
9 Quintus Fabius Maximus, whose delaying tactics had foiled Hannibal.

AENEAS AT THE SITE OF ROME
(*Aeneid* VIII, 310-350)

Around the illustrious stranger darts his sight,
And views each place with wonder and delight:
Curious each ancient monument surveys,
And asks of every work of ancient days,
Half sunk in ruins, and by age o'ercome—
When thus, the founder of majestic Rome:[1]
    "Know, mighty prince, these venerable woods,
Of old were haunted by the silvan gods,
And savage tribes, a rugged race who took

Their birth primeval from the stubborn oak.
No laws, no manners formed the barbarous race;
But wild, the natives roamed from place to place;
Untaught and rough, improvident of gain,
They heaped no wealth, nor turned the fruitful plain.
Their food, the savage fruits the forests yield,
Or hunted game, the fortune of the field,
Till Saturn fled before victorious Jove,
Driven down and banished from the realms above.
He by just laws embodied all the train,
Who roamed the hills, and drew them to the plain;
There stayed, and Latium called the new abode,
Whose friendly shores concealed the hiding god.
These realms in peace the monarch long controlled,
And blessed the nations with an age of gold.
A second age succeeds, but darker far,
Dimmed by the lust of gain, and rage of war.
Then the Sicanians and Ausonians came,
And Saturn's realm alternate changed her name.
Successive tyrants ruled the Latian plain;
Then stern, huge Tybris held his cruel reign.
The mighty flood that bathes the fruitful coast,
Received his name, and Albula was lost.
I came the last, through stormy oceans driven
From my own kingdom by the hand of Heaven.
My mother goddess and Apollo bore
My course at length to this auspicious shore."
　　This said, the prince the gate and altar shows,
That to his parent, great Carmenta, rose;
Whose voice foretold, the sons of Troy should crown
With everlasting fame the rising town.
Here, Pan, beneath the rocks your temple stood;
There, the renowned asylum, in the wood.[2]
Now points the monarch, where by vengeful steel,

His murdered guest, poor, hapless Argus fell!
Next, to the Capitol their course they hold,
Then roofed with reeds, but blazing now with gold.
Even then her awful sanctity appeared:
The swains the local majesty revered.

---

[1] Evander, who had come from Arcadia.
[2] That is, the wood that Romulus turned into an asylum for fugitives.

RECONCILIATION
(*Aeneid* XII, 808-842)

"Great sire, because your sacred will I know,
I left my Turnus to his doom below.[1]
Nor had I sat, but at the will of Jove,
Disgraced and pensive, in the clouds above;
But in the front of fight my foes engaged,
And, wrapt in flames, through all the battle raged.
I bade Juturna mingle in the strife,
Nay, venture more, to save a brother's life.
That charge I own; but not to bend a bow,
Or hurl a single javelin at the foe.
This, this, I swear, by the black Stygian floods,
The sole dread sanction of the immortal gods.
Now back to Heaven, great father, I repair,
And from this hour renounce the hateful war.
But yet I beg, O sovereign of the sky,
What not the hardest laws of fate deny;
For your own Latium I implore this grace,
This honor for your own majestic race:

When by these nuptials both the realms combine,[2]
And in firm leagues of peace and friendship join,
Still may the Latians, still remain the same,
Nor take from Troy their language, garb, or name!
May the great race of Alban monarchs reign,
Kings after kings the regal line sustain;
And from the Italian blood may Rome arise,
In all her pride and glory, to the skies.
But may a long oblivion quite destroy
The last, last ruins, with the name of Troy!"
    The goddess spoke; and with a smile replies
The sire of men, and monarch of the skies:
"Can Saturn's other heir, who reigns above,
The imperial sister, and the wife, of Jove,
With endless schemes of vengeance break her rest?
Why burns such wrath in a celestial breast?
Cease, cease, at length, and lay your anger by,
Since with your wish, my empress, we comply.
The Ausonians ever shall remain the same
In customs, garb, religion, and the name;
And the lost Trojan race forget from whence they came.
In manners, laws, and language, shall they join,
And Ilion shall increase the Latian line.
From hence a pious godlike race shall rise,
The first of men, the darlings of the skies.
Nor all the nations of the world shall pay
More glorious honors to your name, than they."
    Then, pleased and reconciled, the queen of Jove
Flies to her palace, in the realms above.

---

[1] Juno addresses Jupiter.
[2] That is, by the marriage of Aeneas and Lavinia.

THE NEW TESTAMENT

"And it came to pass in those days, that there went out a decree from Caesar Augustus, that all the world should be taxed" (Luke ii, 1). From birth to death, Christ's life was enacted in the context of the Roman Empire; and as J. Westbury-Jones so rightly observed: "One of the most imposing facts in the history of mankind is the contemporaneous establishment of the Empire of the Caesars and the rise of the Kingdom of Jesus Christ. The only two powers which have claimed absolute dominion over mankind appeared together" (p. 1). Moreover, although "Christians vs. Lions" is the picture that has captured the popular imagination, it is evident both that the earliest Christians met more opposition among the Jews than from the Romans, and that Christianity could not have spread so widely so fast had Rome not established a degree of unity in the Mediterranean world.

On the relations between Christianity and the Empire, see J. Westbury-Jones, Roman and Christian Imperialism (London, 1939) Harold Mattingly, Christianity in the Roman Empire (Dunedin, 1955); A. N. Sherwin-White, Roman Society and Roman Law in the New Testament (Oxford, 1963); and J. E. A. Crake, "Early Christians and Roman Law," Phoenix XIX (1965), 61-70.

From The Holy Bible, being the version set forth in A.D. 1611 (Boston & New York: Congregational Publishing Society).

APPEAL UNTO CAESAR
(Acts 25-26)

NOW when Festus[1] was come into the province, after three days he ascended from Caesarea to Jerusalem. Then the high priest and the chief of the Jews informed him against Paul, and besought him, and desired favor against him, that he would send for him to Jerusalem, laying wait in the way to kill him. But Festus answered, that Paul should be kept at Caesarea, and that he himself would depart shortly thither. Let them therefore, said he, which among you are able, go down with me, and accuse this man, if there be any wickedness in him. And when he had tarried among them more than ten days, he went down unto Caesarea; and the next day sitting on the judgment seat commanded Paul to be brought. And when he was come, the Jews which came down from Jerusalem stood round about, and laid many and grievous complaints against Paul, which they could not prove. While he answered for himself, Neither against the law of the Jews, neither against the temple, nor yet against Caesar, have I offended any thing at all. But Festus, willing to do the Jews a pleasure, answered Paul, and said, Wilt thou go up to Jerusalem, and there be judged of these things before me? Then said Paul, I stand at Caesar's judgment seat, where I ought to be judged: to the Jews have I done no wrong, as thou very well knowest. For if I be an offender, or have committed any thing worthy of death, I refuse not to die: but if there be none of these things whereof these accuse me, no man may deliver me unto them. I appeal unto Caesar.[2] Then Festus, when he had conferred with the council, answered, Hast thou appealed unto Caesar? unto Caesar shalt thou go.

And after certain days king Agrippa and Bernice came unto

Caesarea to salute Festus. And when they had been there many days, Festus declared Paul's cause unto the king, saying, There is a certain man left in bonds by Felix: about whom, when I was at Jerusalem, the chief priests and the elders of the Jews informed me, desiring to have judgment against him. To whom I answered, It is not the manner of the Romans to deliver any man to die, before that he which is accused have the accusers face to face, and have licence to answer for himself concerning the crime laid against him. Therefore, when they were come hither, without any delay on the morrow I sat on the judgment seat, and commanded the man to be brought forth. Against whom when the accusers stood up, they brought none accusation of such things as I supposed: but had certain questions against him of their own superstition, and of one Jesus, which was dead, whom Paul affirmed to be alive. And because I doubted of such manner of questions, I asked him whether he would go to Jerusalem, and there be judged of these matters. But when Paul had appealed to be reserved unto the hearing of Augustus, I commanded him to be kept till I might send him to Caesar. Then Agrippa said unto Festus, I would also hear the man myself. To morrow, said he, thou shalt hear him.

And on the morrow, when Agrippa was come, and Bernice with great pomp, and was entered into the place of hearing, with the chief captains, and principal men of the city, at Festus' commandment Paul was brought forth. And Festus said, King Agrippa, and all men which are here present with us, ye see this man, about whom all the multitude of the Jews have dealt with me, both at Jerusalem, and also here, crying that he ought not to live any longer. But when I found that he had committed nothing worthy of death, and that he himself hath appealed to Augustus, I have determined to send him. Of whom I have no certain thing to write unto my lord. Wherefore I have brought him forth before you, and specially before thee, O king Agrippa, that, after examination had, I might have somewhat to write. For it seemed to me unreasonable to send a prisoner, and not withal to signify the crimes laid against him. Then Agrippa said unto Paul, Thou are permitted to speak for thyself. Then Paul stretched forth the hand, and answered for himself:

I think myself happy, king Agrippa, because I shall answer for myself this day before thee touching all the things whereof I am accused of the Jews: especially because I know thee to be expert in all customs and questions which are among the Jews: wherefore I beseech thee to hear me patiently.

My manner of life from my youth, which was at the first mine own nation at Jerusalem, know all the Jews; which knew me from the beginning, if they would testify, that after the most straitest sect of our religion I lived a Pharisee. And now I stand and am judged for the hope of the promise made of God unto our fathers: unto which promise our twelve tribes, instantly serving God day and night, hope to come. For which hope's sake, king Agrippa, I am accused of the Jews. Why should it be thought a thing incredible with you, that God should raise the dead?

I verily thought with myself, that I ought to do many things contrary to the name of Jesus of Nazareth. Which thing I also did in Jerusalem: and many of the saints did I shut up in prison, having received authority from the chief priests; and when they were put to death, I gave my voice against them. And I punished them oft in every synagogue, and compelled them to blaspheme; and being exceedingly mad against them, I persecuted them even unto strange cities.

Whereupon as I went to Damascus with authority and commission from the chief priests, at midday, O king, I saw in the way a light from heaven, above the brightness of the sun, shining round about me and them which journeyed with me. And when we were all fallen to the earth, I heard a voice speaking unto me, and saying in the Hebrew tongue, Saul, Saul, why persecutest thou me? it is hard for thee to kick against the pricks. And I said, Who art thou, Lord, And he said, I am Jesus whom thou persecutest. But rise, and stand upon thy feet: for I have appeared unto thee for this purpose, to make thee a minister and a witness both of these things which thou hast seen, and of those things in the which I will appear unto thee; delivering thee from the people, and from the Gentiles, unto whom now I send thee, to open their eyes, and to turn them from darkness to light, and from the power of Satan unto God, that they may receive forgiveness of sins, and inheritance among them which are sanctified by faith that is in me.

Whereupon, O king Agrippa, I was not disobedient unto the heavenly vision: but shewed first unto them of Damascus, and at Jerusalem, and throughout all the coasts of Judaea, and then to the Gentiles, that they should repent and turn to God, and do works meet for repentance. For these causes the Jews caught me in the temple, and went about to kill me. Having therefore obtained help of God, I continue unto this day, witnessing both to small and great, saying none other things than those which the prophets and Moses did say should come: that Christ should suffer, and that he should be the first that should rise from the dead, and should shew light unto the people, and to the Gentiles.

And as he thus spake for himself, Festus said with a loud voice, Paul, thou art beside thyself; much learning doth make thee mad. But he said, I am not mad, most noble Festus; but speak forth the words of truth and soberness. For the king knoweth of these things, before whom also I speak freely: for I am persuaded that none of these things are hidden from him; for this thing was not done in a corner.

King Agrippa, believest thou the prophets? I know that thou believest. Then Agrippa said unto Paul, Almost thou persuadest me to be a Christian. And Paul said, I would to God, that not only thou, but also all that hear me this day, were both almost, and altogether such as I am, except these bonds.

And when he had thus spoken, the king rose up, and the governor, and Bernice, and they that sat with them: and when they were gone aside, they talked between themselves, saying, This man doeth nothing worthy of death or of bonds. Then said Agrippa unto Festus, This man might have been set at liberty, if he had not appealed unto Caesar.[3]

---

[1] He had succeeded Felix as governor of Judaea. Caesarea was the Roman, Jerusalem the Jewish capital.

[2] An appeal to the emperor was open only to Roman citizens, who were immune from scourging (cf. Acts 22:25-29) and crucifixion (they were beheaded instead).

[3] Paul's trial took place in 59, and the next year he reached Rome, where he was under open arrest for two years. Upon his release he revisited Greece and Asia Minor. Nero began his persecution of Christians in 64, the year of the Great Fire of Rome; and tradition has it that both Peter and Paul were martyred there in 67. Luke's account probably was composed during the period of Paul's initial imprisonment at Rome.

BABYLON THE GREAT
(Revelation 17-18)

AND there came one of the seven angels which had the seven vials, and talked with me, saying unto me, Come hither; I will shew unto thee the judgment of the great whore that sitteth upon many waters: with whom the kings of the earth have committed fornication and the inhabitants of the earth have been made drunk with the wine of her fornication.[1] So he carried me away in the spirit into the wilderness: and I saw a woman sit upon a scarlet colored beast, full of names of blasphemy, having seven heads and ten horns. And the woman was arrayed in purple and scarlet color, and decked with gold and precious stones and pearls, having a golden cup in her hand full of abominations and filthiness of her fornication: and upon her forehead was a name written, MYSTERY, BABYLON THE GREAT, THE MOTHER OF HARLOTS AND ABOMINATIONS OF THE EARTH. And I saw the woman drunken with the blood of the martyrs of Jesus: and when I saw her, I wondered with great admiration. And the angel said unto me, Wherefore didst thou marvel? I will tell thee the mystery of the woman, and of the beast that carrieth her, which hath the seven heads and ten horns.

The beast that thou sawest was, and is not; and shall ascend out of the bottomless pit, and go into perdition: and they that dwell on the earth shall wonder, whose names were not written in the book of life from the foundation of the world, when they behold the beast that was, and is not, and yet is. And here is the mind which hath wisdom. The seven heads are seven mountains, on which the woman sitteth. And there are seven kings: five are fallen, and one is, and the other is not yet to come; and when he cometh, he must continue a short space. And the beast that was, and is not, even he is the eighth, and is of the seven, and goeth into perdition. And the ten horns which thou sawest are ten kings, which have received no kingdom as yet; but receive power as kings one hour with the beast. These have one mind, and shall give their power and strength unto the beast. These shall make war with the Lamb, and the Lamb shall overcome them: for he is Lord of lords, and King of kings: and they that are with him are called, and chosen, and faithful. And he saith unto me, The waters which thou sawest, where the whore sitteth, are peoples, and multitudes, and nations, and tongues. And the ten horns which thou sawest upon the beast, these shall hate the whore, and shall make her desolate and naked, and shall eat her flesh, and burn her with fire. For God hath put in their hearts to fulfill his will, and to agree, and give their kingdom unto the beast, until the words of God shall be fulfilled. And the woman which thou sawest is that great city, which reigneth over the kings of the earth.

And after these things I saw another angel come down from heaven, having great power; and the earth was lightened with his glory. And he cried mightily with a strong voice, saying, Babylon the great is fallen, is fallen, and is become the habitation of devils, and the hold of every foul spirit, and a cage of every unclean and hateful bird. For all nations have drunk of the wine of the wrath of her fornication, and the kings of the earth have committed fornication with her, and the merchants of the earth are waxed rich through the abundance of her delicacies. And I heard another voice from heaven, saying, Come out of her, my people, that ye be not partakers of her sins, and that ye receive not of her plagues. For her sins have reached unto heaven, and God hath remembered her iniquities. Reward her even as she rewarded you, and double unto her double according to her works: in the cup which she hath filled fill to her double. How much she hath glorified herself, and lived deliciously, so much torment and sorrow give her: for she saith in her heart, I sit a queen, and am no widow, and shall see no sorrow. Therefore shall her plagues come in one day, death, and mourning, and famine; and she shall be utterly burned with fire: for strong is the Lord God who judgeth her. And the kings of earth, who have committed fornication and lived deliciously with her, shall bewail her, and lament for her, when they shall see the smoke of her burning. Standing afar off for the fear of her torment, saying, Alas, alas that great city Babylon, that mighty city! for in one hour is thy judgment come. And the merchants of the earth shall weep and mourn over her; for no man buyeth their merchandise any more: the merchandise of gold, and silver, and precious stones, and of pearls, and fine linen, and purple, and silk, and scarlet, and all thyine wood, and all manner vessels of most precious wood, and of brass, and iron, and marble, and cinnamon, and odors, and ointments, and frankincense, and wine, and oil, and fine flour, and wheat, and beasts, and sheep, and horses, and chariots, and slaves, and souls of men. And the fruits that thy soul lusted after are departed from thee, and all things which were dainty and goodly are departed from thee, and thou shalt find them no more at all. The merchants of these things, which were made rich by her, shall stand afar off for the fear of her torment, weeping and wailing, and saying, Alas, alas that great city, that was clothed in fine linen, and purple, and scarlet, and decked with gold, and precious stones, and pearls! For in one hour so great riches is come to nought. And every shipmaster, and all the company in ships, and sailors, and as many as trade by sea, stood afar off, and cried when they saw the smoke of her burning, saying, What city is like unto this great city! And they cast dust on their heads, and cried, weeping and wailing, saying, Alas, alas that great city, wherein were made rich all that had ships in the sea by reason of her costliness! for in one hour is she made desolate.

Rejoice over her, thou heaven, and ye holy apostles and prophets; for God hath avenged you on her.

And a mighty angel took up a stone like a great millstone, and cast it into the sea, saying, Thus with violence shall that great city Babylon be thrown down, and shall be found no more at all. And the voice of harpers, and musicians, and of pipers, and trumpeters, shall be heard no more at all in thee; and no craftsman, of whatsoever craft he be, shall be found any more in thee; and the sound of a millstone shall be heard no more at all in thee; and the light of a candle shall shine no more at all in thee; and the voice of the bridegroom and of the bride shall be heard no more at all in thee; for thy merchants were the great

men of the earth; for by thy sorceries were all nations deceived.
And in her was found the blood of prophets, and of saints, and
of all that were slain upon the earth.

1 This apocalyptic vision was probably composed during persecutions in the
reign of Domitian (81-96), the first ruler since Caligula who seriously enforced the cult of the emperor, which had a number of affinities with
Christianity (about which see E. F. Scott, "The Opposition to Caesar Worship," in *Church History* II, no. 2). On the complex symbolism of the work
see Martin Kiddle, *The Revelation of St. John* (New York & London, 1941),
who identifies Babylon with the Empire rather than just the city of Rome.

TACITUS

In provincial areas, the Roman citizenship was first extended on a large scale under Caesar and Augustus. At the outbreak of the Civil War (49 B.C.), Caesar himself had enfranchised the Gallic population north of the Po; and about a century later Claudius, who was born at Lugdunum, "shattered the opinion that the Roman state knew boundaries determined by any other considerations than her own power of absorption and attraction" (Sherwin-White, p. 192).

Large fragments of Claudius' speech were discovered at Lyon in 1524; and from this Tabula Lugdunensis we can see how Tacitus has re-written, condensed and improved upon the emperor's argument. But since such set speeches were a prominent feature of ancient historical writing, even where the author could have no way of knowing what, if anything, had actually been said (as was certainly the case with the British chieftain, Calgacus), he would devise a speech expressing what could—or should—have been uttered on such an occasion.

See A. N. Sherwin-White, The Roman Citizenship (Oxford, 1939); Ronald Syme, Tacitus, 2 volumes (Oxford, 1958), especially "Tacitus and Gaul" (I, 451-463); and E. Birley, Roman Britain and the Roman Army: Collected Papers (Kendal, 1953).

From The Works of Tacitus, The Oxford Translation, Revised, 2 volumes (London: Bohn, 1854).

GAULS IN THE SENATE

(*Annals* XI, 23-24)

IN THE consulship of Aulus Vitellius and Lucius Vipsanius,[1] when the business of supplying the vacancies in the senate was in agitation, and the nobility of that part of Gaul called Comata, who had long since acquired the distinction of confederates and citizens of Rome, now sued for a participation of offices and honors; many and various were the reasonings of the public upon their pretensions, and eager were the efforts of the opposite parties to influence the mind of the prince: he was told, "that Italy was not fallen so low that she could not furnish a supply of senators to her own capital. Of old her natives sufficed for recruiting the people who were of the same blood with themselves: nor was there any cause for condemning the institutions of the ancient republic. Nay, even at this day, examples of virtue and renown were referred to, which the Roman genius had produced under her ancient institutions. Was it not enough that the Venetae and Insubrians had invaded the senate, but that a host of foreigners, like a band of captives, must be introduced? What distinctions would remain to the old nobility? or to any poor senator from Latium? All public honors would be engrossed by those opulent Gauls; whose fathers and forefathers, at the head of hostile nations, opposed and slaughtered our armies, and at Alesia besieged the sainted Julius: instances these of later days; but what if the recollection should flash across the mind, of those who fell before the capitol and citadel of Rome by the hands of these same men? They might, in truth, still enjoy the title of citizens; but not profane the honors of the senatorian rank, or the splendors of the magistracy."

The emperor, little affected by these and similar allegations, answered them off hand; and then summoning the senate, thus addressed them: "My ancestors, the oldest of whom, Attus Clausus, though of Sabine origin, was at once enrolled among Roman citizens, and adopted into the patrician rank, furnish me with a lesson that I ought to pursue similar measures in directing the affairs of the commonwealth, and transfer to Rome everything that is of preeminent merit wheresoever found. Nor indeed am I ignorant that from Alba we had the Julii, from Camerium the Coruncanii, and the Porcii from Tusculum: and not to enter into a minute detail of remote transactions, that from Etruria, Lucania, and all Italy, persons have been incorporated into the senate. At last our city became bounded only by the Alps; so that not only separate individuals, but whole states and nations, became ingrafted into the Roman name. We had solid peace at home, and our arms prospered abroad, when the nations beyond the Po were presented with the rights of citizens; and when under pretext of leading out legions into colonies all over the earth, and uniting with them the flower of the natives, we recruited our exhausted state. Do we regret that the Balbi migrated to us from Spain, or men equally illustrious from the Narbon Gaul? Their descendants remain yet with us, nor yield to us in their love of this our common country. What proved the bane of the Spartans and Athenians, though potent in arms, but that they treated as aliens and refused to unite with the conquered? On the other hand, so great was the wisdom of Romulus, our founder, that he saw several people his enemies and his citizens, in one and the same day. Foreigners have ever reigned over us. For magistracies to be intrusted to the children of freemen is no innovation, as many are erroneously persuaded, but a constant practice of the elder people. But, it is urged, we have had wars with the Senones: have the Volscians, have the Aequians never engaged us in battle? It is true, our capital has been taken by the

Gauls; but by the Tuscans we have been forced to give hostages; and by the Samnites to pass under the yoke. However, upon a review of all our wars, none will be found to have been more speedily concluded than that with the Gauls; and from that time uninterrupted peace has existed: identified with us in customs, in civil and military accomplishments, and domestic alliances; let them rather introduce amongst us their gold and wealth, than enjoy them without our participation. All the institutions, conscript fathers, which are now venerated as most ancient, were once new: the plebeian magistrates were later than the patricians; the Latin later than the plebeian; those of other nations in Italy came after the Latin: the present admission of the Gauls will also wax old; and what is this day supported by precedents, will hereafter become a precedent."

[1]A.D. 48. Vitellius is the future emperor.

BENEFITS OF ROMAN RULE
(*Histories* IV, 73-74)

CEREALIS then called an assembly of the Treverians and Lingones,[1] and thus addressed them: "Eloquence, indeed, is a talent which I never cultivated. In the field of battle I have manifested the character of the Roman people for valor. But as words weigh with you more than anything, and things good and evil are estimated by you, not with reference to their intrinsic merits, but the coloring of incendiaries, I have resolved to address a few words to you, which, now the war is over, it will be more your interest to have heard, than mine to have uttered. The Roman generals and emperors entered your territories, and

the other provinces of Gaul, from no lust of conquest, but solicited by your ancestors, at that time torn by intestine divisions,
and driven to the brink of ruin; and when the Germans, whom
you called to your aid, enslaved, without distinction, those who
invited them, and those who resisted. The battles which Rome
has fought with the Teutons and the Cimbrians,—her wars in
Germany, and the toil and vigor of her legions, with the various
events that followed, are all sufficiently known. If our legions
were posted on the banks of the Rhine, it was not for the
defence of Italy, but lest another Ariovistus should aspire to
reign over you. And do you now imagine that Civilis, or the
Batavians, or the nations beyond the Rhine, have that affection
for you and your welfare which your forefathers never experienced from their ancestors? The same motives that first incited
the Germans to cross the Rhine, will ever subsist: ambition,
avarice, and the love of new settlements: ready, at all times, to
change their swampy fens and barren deserts to get possession
of your fertile plains and yourselves. But liberty and specious
pretences are employed to veil their designs; nor did ever any
man desire to reduce others to servitude and subjection to himself, without using the same terms.

"Your country, till you put yourselves under our protection,
was at all times harassed with wars, and oppressed by tyrants.
Rome, though so often provoked by war, imposed upon you by
the right of conquest that only which was necessary to preserve
peace. For to maintain the tranquillity of nations, arms are
necessary; soldiers must be kept in pay; and without a tribute
supplies cannot be raised. All other things are placed upon a
footing of equality. Our legions are often commanded by you;
you are governors of your own provinces, and even of others.
Nothing is reserved to ourselves, no exclusiveness exercised.
Does a virtuous prince reign at Rome? though placed at a distance, you feel the mildness of his government equally with
ourselves. Tyrants turn their rage upon those immediately

within their reach. In the same manner as you submit to excessive rains, and barren seasons, and all the other calamities of nature, so also put up with the avarice and prodigality of princes. As long as human nature remains there will be faults. But even these are not unvaried; but are compensated by the occasional display of better qualities. Unless, perhaps, you expect from Tutor and Classicus a milder and more equitable reign; or that under their auspices armies will be raised to repel the Germans and the Britons, by means of lighter tributes than are now paid. For if the Roman dominion is repudiated, (which may the gods avert!) what other consequence will result than that all the nations will be engaged in war with each other? During a space of eight hundred years, this fabric of empire has been raised by good fortune and strict discipline; nor can it be torn down without bringing ruin upon its destroyers. But you will be exposed to the greatest danger. You have gold and riches, those great incentives to war. Cherish, therefore, and honor peace and the city of Rome: a city whose privileges you enjoy, alike the conquerer and the conquered. Let the experience you have had of the vicissitudes of fortune instruct you to prefer submission with security to rebellion with ruin." Such was the speech with which he allayed the fears, and revived the hopes of the Gauls, who apprehended severer treatment.

---

[1] After Vitellius was slain at the end of A.D. 69, the Batavian chief Civilis attacked the Romans; and an "Empire of the Gauls" was promoted by the chieftains of the Treveri and Lingones (Tutor was a Treverian whom Vitellius had made a commander on the banks of the Rhine). Syme observes: "The lesson was not lost. The next age does not show many senators from Tres Galliae" (I, 462).

ROMAN RAPACITY
(*Agricola* 30-32)

"WHEN I reflect on the causes of the war, and the circumstances of our situation, I feel a strong persuasion that our
united efforts on the present day will prove the beginning of
universal liberty to Britain.[1] For we are all undebased by slavery;
and there is no land behind us, nor does even the sea afford a
refuge, whilst the Roman fleet hovers around. Thus the use of
arms, which is at all times honorable to the brave, now offers
the only safety even to cowards. In all the battles which have
yet been fought, with various success, against the Romans, our
countrymen may be deemed to have reposed their final hopes
and resources in us: for we, the noblest sons of Britain, and
therefore stationed in its last recesses, far from the view of
servile shores, have preserved even our eyes unpolluted by the
contact of subjection. We, at the furthest limits both of land
and liberty, have been defended to this day by the remoteness of
our situation and of our fame. The extremity of Britain is now
disclosed; and whatever is unknown becomes an object of magnitude. But there is no nation beyond us; nothing but waves
and rocks, and the still more hostile Romans, whose arrogance
we cannot escape by obsequiousness and submission. These
plunderers of the world, after exhausting the land by their
devastations, are rifling the ocean: stimulated by avarice, if
their enemy be rich; by ambition, if poor: unsatiated by the
East and by the West: the only people who behold wealth and
indigence with equal avidity. To ravage, to slaughter, to usurp
under false titles, they call empire; and where they make a
desert, they call it peace.

"Our children and relations are by the appointment of nature the dearest of all things to us. These are torn away by

levies to serve in foreign lands. Our wives and sisters, though
they should escape the violation of hostile force, are polluted
under names of friendship and hospitality. Our estates and
possessions are consumed in tributes; our grain in contributions. Even our bodies are worn down amidst stripes and insults in clearing woods and draining marshes. Wretches born
to slavery are once bought, and afterwards maintained by their
masters: Britain every day buys, every day feeds, her own
servitude. And as among domestic slaves every new comer
serves for the scorn and derision of his fellows; so, in this ancient household of the world, we, as the newest and vilest, are
sought out to destruction. For we have neither cultivated
lands, nor mines, nor harbors, which can induce them to preserve us for our labors. The valor too and unsubmitting spirit
of subjects only render them more obnoxious to their masters;
while remoteness and secrecy of situation itself, in proportion
as it conduces to security, tends to inspire suspicion. Since
then all hopes of mercy are vain, at length assume courage,
both you to whom safety and you to whom glory is dear. The
Trinobantes, even under a female leader, had force enough to
burn a colony, to storm camps, and, if success had not damped
their vigor, would have been able entirely to throw off the
yoke; and shall not we, untouched, unsubdued, and struggling
not for the acquisition but the security of liberty, show at the
very first onset what men Caledonia has reserved for her
defence?

"Can you imagine that the Romans are as brave in war as
they are licentious in peace? Acquiring renown from our dis-
cords and dissensions, they convert the faults of their enemies
to the glory of their own army; an army compounded of the
most different nations, which success alone had kept together,
and which misfortune will as certainly dissipate. Unless, indeed, you can suppose that Gauls, and Germans, and (I blush
to say it) even Britons, who, though they expend their blood

to establish a foreign dominion, have been longer its foes than its subjects, will be retained by loyalty and affection! Terror and dread alone are the weak bonds of attachment; which once broken, they who cease to fear will begin to hate. Every incitement to victory is on our side. The Romans have no wives to animate them; no parents to upbraid their flight. Most of them have either no home, or a distant one. Few in number, ignorant of the country, looking around in silent horror at woods, seas, and a heaven itself unknown to them, they are delivered by the gods, as it were imprisoned and bound, into our hands. Be not terrified with an idle show, and the glitter of silver and gold, which can neither protect nor wound. In the very ranks of the enemy we shall find our own bands. The Britons will acknowledge their own cause. The Gauls will recollect their former liberty. The rest of the Germans will desert them, as the Usipii have lately done. Nor is there anything formidable behind them: ungarrisoned forts; colonies of old men; municipal towns distempered and distracted between unjust masters and ill-obeying subjects. Here is a general; here an army. There, tributes, mines, and all the train of punishments inflicted on slaves; which whether to bear eternally, or instantly to revenge, this field must determine. March then to battle, and think of your ancestors and your posterity."[2]

---

[1] A British chief, Calgacus, is exhorting his men before the battle of Mons Graupius (A.D. 84).

[2] The Britons were routed by an army under Julius Agricola, Tacitus' father-in-law. Agricola's father was from the province Narbonensis; Agricola himself was educated at Massilia (Marseille); and Syme sees implied in the Agricola "a vindication of the new men from the provinces, setting them up against effete aristocrats and the parochial Italians" (I, 29). Cf. Fergus Millar, The Roman Empire and its Neighbors (New York, 1968), one of whose themes is "the gradual replacement of a distinction between local groups (Roman citizens, predominantly Italians—and others) by one applicable, as far as we know, equally over the whole Empire, between classes."

AELIUS ARISTIDES

Chester Starr has observed that "the rise of the equation Empire-Justice to the limelight would appear to reflect the rise of the provinces to that position of essential equality which they gained by the time of Hadrian" (pp. 14-15). The warmest proponent of this view was a Greek sophist whose ceremonial oration in praise of Rome probably dates from A.D. 143. Of his work James Oliver remarks that "Aelius Aristides of course knew the record of the old (so-called libera) res publica. To most Greeks it appeared just another tyrant city, and the less said about it the better. Aristides emphasizes the wonderful transformation under the emperors" (p. 894). Indeed, Aristides goes a step beyond even Virgil: he ignores all of Rome's early history and reproves Hesiod for placing the Golden Age in the past, instead of foreseeing that it would begin with the advent of the Roman Empire.

See Chester G. Starr, "The Perfect Democracy of the Roman Empire," American Historical Review LVIII (1952), 1-16; William E. Heitland, "Discussion of Certain Ancient Panegyrics on the Roman Empire," in Last Words on the Roman Municipalities (Cambridge, 1928), pp. 64-80; R. W. Livingstone, The Mission of Greece: Some Greek Views of Life in the Roman World (Oxford, 1928); and James H. Oliver, "The Ruling Power: A Study of the Roman Empire in the Second Century after Christ through the Roman Oration of Aelius Aristides," Transactions of the American Philosophical Society, New Series, Volume 43, Part 4 (1953), pp. 871-1003 (from which the following selections are reprinted with the permission of Professor Oliver and of the American Philosophical Society).

THE CITY OF ROME
(*Roman Oration* 7-12)

HOMER says of snow that as it falls, it covers "the crest of the range and the mountain peaks and the flowering fields and the rich acres of men, and," he says, "it is poured out over the white sea, the harbors and the shores."[1] So also of this city. Like the snow, she covers mountain peaks, she covers the land intervening, and she goes down to the sea, where the commerce of all mankind has its common exchange and all the produce of the earth has its common market. Wherever one may go in Rome, there is no vacancy to keep one from being, there also, in mid-city. And indeed she is poured out, not just over the level ground, but in a manner with which the simile cannot begin to keep pace, she rises great distances into the air, so that her height is not to be compared to a covering of snow but rather to the peaks themselves. And as a man who far surpasses others in size and strength likes to show his strength by carrying others on his back, so this city, which is built over so much land, is not satisfied with her extent, but raising upon her shoulders others of equal size, one over the other, she carries them. It is from this that she gets her name, and strength (rômê) is the mark of all that is hers. Therefore, if one chose to unfold, as it were, and lay flat on the ground the cities which she now carries high in air, and place them side by side, all that part of Italy which intervenes would, I think, be filled and become one continuous city stretching to the Strait of Otranto.

Though she is so vast as perhaps even now I have not sufficiently shown, but as the eye attests more clearly, it is not possible to say of her as of other cities, "There she stands." Again it has been said of the capital cities of the Athenians and the Lacedaemonians—and may no ill omen attend the comparison—that the first would in size appear twice as great as in its intrinsic power, the second far inferior in size to its intrinsic power. But of this city, great in every respect, no one could say that she has not created power in keeping with her magnitude. No, if one looks at the whole empire and reflects how small a fraction rules the whole world, he may be amazed at the city, but when he has beheld the city herself and the boundaries of the city, he can no longer be amazed that the entire civilized world is ruled by one so great.

Some chronicler, speaking of Asia, asserted that one man ruled as much land as the sun passed, and his statement was not true because he placed all Africa and Europe outside the limits where the sun rises in the East and sets in the West. It has now however turned out to be true. Your possession is equal to what the sun can pass, and the sun passes over your land. Neither the Chelidonean nor the Cyanean promontories limit your empire, nor does the distance from which a horseman can reach the sea in one day, nor do you reign within fixed boundaries, nor does another dictate to what point your control reaches; but the sea like a girdle lies extended, at once in the middle of the civlized world and of your hegemony.

Around it lie the great continents greatly sloping, ever offering to you in full measure something of their own. Whatever the seasons make grow and whatever countries and rivers and lakes and arts of Hellenes and non-Hellenes produce are brought from every land and sea, so that if one would look at all these things, he must needs behold them either by visiting the entire civilized world or by coming to this city. For whatever is grown and made among each people cannot fail to be here at all times and in abundance. And here the merchant vessels come carrying these many products from all regions in every season and even at every equinox, so that the city appears a kind of common emporium of the world. Cargoes from India and, if you will, even from Arabia the Blest one can see in such numbers as to surmise that in those lands the trees will have been stripped bare and that the inhabitants of these lands, if they need anything, must come here and beg for a share of their own. Again one can see Babylonian garments and ornaments from the barbarian country beyond arriving in greater quantity and with more ease than if shippers from Naxos or from Cythnos, bearing something from those islands, had but to enter the port of Athens. Your farms are Egypt, Sicily and the civilized part of Africa.[2]

[1] *Iliad* XII, 281-284.
[2] On the cosmopolitanism of the era, see Clifford H. Moore, "The Decay of Nationalism under the Roman Empire," *Transactions and Proceedings of the American Philological Association* XLVIII (1917), 27-36.

THE ROMAN EMPIRE
(*Roman Oration* 29, 31-37)

VAST and comprehensive as is the size of it, your empire is much greater for its perfection than for the area which its boundaries encircle. There are no pockets of the empire held by Mysians, Sacae, Pisidians, or others, land which some have occupied by force, others have detached by revolt, who cannot be captured. Nor is it merely called the land of the *King*, while really the land of all who are able to hold it. Nor do satraps fight one another as if they had no king; nor are cities at variance, some fighting against these and some against those, with garrisons being dispatched to some cities and being expelled from others. But for the eternal duration of this empire the whole civilized world prays all together, emitting, like an aulos after a thorough cleaning, one note with more perfect precision

than a chorus; so beautifully is it harmonized by the leader in
command. . . . All directions are carried out by the chorus
of the civilized world at a word or gesture of guidance more
easily than at some plucking of a chord; and if anything need
be done, it suffices to decide and there it is already done.

The governors sent out to the city-states and ethnic groups
are each of them rulers of those under them, but in what con-
cerns themselves and their relations to each other they are all
equally among the ruled, and in particular they differ from
those under their rule in that it is they—one might assert—who
first show how to be the right kind of subject. So much respect
has been instilled in all men for him who is the great governor,
who obtains for them their all.

They think that he knows what they are doing better than
they do themselves. Accordingly they fear his displeasure and
stand in greater awe of him than one would of a despot, a master who was present and watching and uttering commands. No
one is so proud that he can fail to be moved upon hearing even
the mere mention of the Ruler's name, but, rising, he praises
and worships him and breathes two prayers in a single breath,
one to the gods on the Ruler's behalf, one for his own affairs
to the Ruler himself. And if the governors should have even
some slight doubt whether certain claims are valid in connection with either public or private lawsuits and petitions from
the governed, they straightway send to him with a request for
instructions what to do, and they wait until he renders a reply,
like a chorus waiting for its trainer.

Therefore, he has no need to wear himself out traveling
around the whole empire, nor, by appearing personally, now
among some, then among others, to make sure of each point
when he has the time to tread their soil. It is very easy for him
to stay where he is and manage the entire civilized world by
letters, which arrive almost as soon as they are written, as if
they were carried by winged messengers.

But that which deserves as much wonder and admiration as all the rest together, and constant expression of gratitude both in word and action, shall now be mentioned. You who hold so vast an empire and rule it with such a firm hand and with so much unlimited power have very decidedly won a great success, which is completely your own.

For of all who have ever gained empire you alone rule over men who are free. Caria has not been given to Tissaphernes, nor Phrygia to Pharnabazus, nor Egypt to someone else; nor is the country said to be enslaved, as household of so-and-so, to whomsoever it has been turned over, a man himself not free. But just as those in states of one city appoint the magistrates to protect and care for the governed, so you, who conduct public business in the whole civilized world exactly as if it were one city state, appoint the governors, as is natural after elections, to protect and care for the governed, not to be slave masters over them. Therefore governor makes way for governor unobtrusively, when his time is up, and far from staying too long and disputing the land with his successor, he might easily not stay long enough even to meet him. Appeals to a higher court are made with the ease of an appeal from deme to dicastery, with no greater menace for those who make them than for those who have accepted the local verdict. Therefore one might say that the men of today are ruled by the governors who are sent out, only in so far as they are content to be ruled.

THE ROMAN CITIZENSHIP
(*Roman Oration* 59-71a)

BUT there is that which very decidedly deserves as much attention and admiration now as all the rest together. I mean

your magnificent citizenship with its grand conception, because there is nothing like it in all the records of mankind.
Dividing into two groups all those in your empire—and with
this word I have indicated the entire civilized world—you have
everywhere appointed to your citizenship, or even to kinship
with you, the better part of the world's talent, courage, and
leadership, while the rest you recognized as a league under your
hegemony.[1]

Neither sea nor intervening continent are bars to citizenship,
nor are Asia and Europe divided in their treatment here. In
your empire all paths are open to all. No one worthy of rule or
trust remains an alien, but a civil community of the World has
been established as a Free Republic under one, the best, ruler
and teacher of order; and all come together as into a common
civic center, in order to receive each man his due.

What another city is to its own boundaries and territory, this
city is to the boundaries and territory of the entire civilized
world, as if the latter were a country district and she had been
appointed common town. It might be said that this one citadel
is the refuge and assembly place of all perioeci or of all who
dwell in outside demes.

She has never failed them, but like the soil of the earth, she
supports all men; and as the sea, which receives with its gulfs
all the many rivers, hides them and holds them all and still,
with what goes in and out, is and seems ever the same, so actually this city receives those who flow in from all the earth and
has even sameness in common with the sea. The latter is not
made greater by the influx of rivers, for it has been ordained by
fate that with the waters flowing in, the sea maintain its volume;
here no change is visible because the city is so great.

Let this passing comment, which the subject suggested, suffice. As we were saying, you who are "great greatly" distributed
your citizenship. It was not because you stood off and refused to
give a share in it to any of the others that you made your citizen-

ship an object of wonder. On the contrary, you sought its expansion as a worthy aim, and you have caused the word Roman to be the label, not of membership in a city, but of some common nationality, and this not just one among all, but one balancing all the rest. For the categories into which you now divide the world are not Hellenes and Barbarians, and it is not absurd, the distinction which you made, because you show them a citizenry more numerous, so to speak, than the entire Hellenic race. The division which you substituted is one into Roman and non-Roman. To such a degree have you expanded the name of your city.

Since these are the lines along which the distinction has been made, many in every city are fellow-citizens of yours no less than of their own kinsmen, though some of them have not yet seen this city. There is no need of garrisons to hold their citadels, but the men of greatest standing and influence in every city guard their own fatherlands for you. And you have a double hold upon the cities, both from here and from your fellow citizens in each.

No envy sets foot in the empire, for you yourselves were the first to disown envy, when you placed all opportunities in view of all and offered those who were able a chance to be not governed more than they governed in turn. Nor does hatred either steal in from those who are not chosen. For since the constitution is a universal one and, as it were, of one state, naturally your governors rule not as over the property of others but as over their own. Besides, all the masses have as a share in it the permission to take refuge with you from the power of the local magnates, but there is the indignation and punishment from you which will come upon them immediately, if they themselves dare to make any unlawful charge.

Thus the present regime naturally suits and serves both rich and poor. No other way of life is left. There has developed in your constitution a single harmonious, all-embracing union; and what formerly seemed to be impossible has come to pass in your time: maintenance of control over an empire, over a vast one at that, and at the same time firmness of rule without unkindness.

Thus the cities can be clear of garrisons. Mere detachments of horse and foot suffice for the protection of whole countries, and even these are not concentrated in the cities with billets in every household, but are dispersed throughout the rural area within bounds and orbits of their own. Hence many nations do not know where at any time their guardians are. But if anywhere a city through excess of growth had passed beyond the ability to maintain order by itself, you did not begrudge to these in their turn the men to stand by and guard them carefully.

It is not safe for those to rule who have not power. The second best way to sail, they say, is to be governed by one's betters, but by you now it has been shown to be actually the first best way. Accordingly, all are held fast and would not ask to secede any more than those at sea from the helmsman. As bats in caves cling fast to each other and to the rocks, so all from you depend with much concern not to fall from this cluster of cities, and would sooner conceive fear of being abandoned by you, than abandon you themselves. And as a result all send their tribute to you with more pleasure than some would actually receive it from others: they have good reason.

They no longer dispute over the right to rule and to have first honors, which caused the outbreak of all the wars of the past. Instead, the rulers of yore do not even recall with certainty what domain they once had, while the others, like water in silent flow, are most delightfully at rest. They have gladly ceased from toil and trouble, for they have come to realize that in the other case they were fighting vainly over shadows. As in the myth of a Pamphylian, or if not so, then Plato's myth,[2] the cities, already being laid, at it were, upon the funeral pyre by their mutual strife and disorder, merely received the right leadership all at once and suddenly revived. How they reached this point they have no explanation and can only wonder at the present. They have come to feel like men aroused from sleep: instead of the dreams they but recently had, they awakened to the sudden vision and presence of these genuine blessings.

Wars, even if they once occurred, no longer seem to have been real; on the contrary, stories about them are interpreted more as myths by the many who hear them. If anywhere an actual clash occurs along the border, as is only natural in the immensity of a great empire, because of the madness of Getae or the misfortune of Libyans or the wickedness of those around the Red Sea, who are unable to enjoy the blessings they have, then simply like myths they themselves quickly pass and the stories about them. So great is your peace, though war was traditional among you.

1 It was not until A.D. 212, with the Edict of Caracalla, that Roman citizenship was extended to all free inhabitants of the empire (except a limited group), apparently for motives more fiscal than ecumenical.
2 *Republic* X, 613-621 (the myth of Er, who revived after having been placed on the funeral pyre).

EDWARD GIBBON

"It was at Rome," Gibbon tells us in his autobiography, "on the 15th of October, 1764, as I sat musing amidst the ruins of the Capitol, while the barefooted friars were singing vespers in the Temple of Jupiter, that the idea of writing the decline and fall of the city first started to my mind." Begun four years later, the work was completed—down to the fall of Constantinople, for Gibbon had since widened his scope—in 1787 and published the following year.

Gibbon's reference to the barefooted friars tells us much about his views; for despite an avowed confidence in human progress he believed that "If a man were called to fix the period in the history of the world during which the condition of the human race was most happy and prosperous, he would, without hesitation, name that which elapsed from the death of Domitian to the accession of Commodus" (chapter 3).

For a recent assessment of Gibbon within the context of his times, see Andrew Lossky's "Introduction: Gibbon and the Enlightenment," in The Transformation of the Roman World: Gibbon's Problem after Two Centuries, ed. Lynn White, Jr. (Berkeley & Los Angeles, 1966), pp. 1-29. On Gibbon as an historian: A. D. Momigliano, "Gibbon's Contribution to Historical Method," reprinted in Studies in Historiography (London, 1966), pp. 40-55.

From The History of the Decline and Fall of the Roman Empire, ed. Bury, volume I (New York: Fred de Fan, 1906). Gibbon's and Bury's notes have been omitted.

THE GREATNESS OF ROME
(*The Decline and Fall of the*
Roman Empire, Ch. 2)

IT IS not by the rapidity or extent of conquest that we should estimate the greatness of Rome. The sovereign of the Russian deserts commands a larger portion of the globe. In the seventh summer after his passage of the Hellespont, Alexander erected the Macedonian trophies on the banks of the Hyphasis. Within less than a century, the irresistible Zingis, and the Mogul princes of his race, spread their cruel devastations and transient empire from the sea of China to the confines of Egypt and Germany. But the firm edifice of Roman power was raised and preserved by the wisdom of the ages. The obedient provinces of Trajan and the Antonines were united by laws and adorned by arts. They might occasionally suffer from the partial abuse of delegated authority; but the general principle of government was wise, simple, and beneficent. They enjoyed the religion of their ancestors, whilst in civil honors and advantages they were exalted, by just degrees, to an equality with their conquerers.

The policy of the emperors and the senate, as far as it concerned religion, was happily seconded by the reflections of the enlightened, and by the habits of the superstitious, part of their subjects. The various modes of worship which prevailed in the Roman world were all considered by the people as equally true; by the philosopher as equally false; and by the magistrate as equally useful. And thus toleration produced not only mutual indulgence, but even religious concord.

The superstition of the people was not embittered by any mixture of theological rancor; nor was it confined by the chains of any speculative system. The devout polytheist, though fondly attached to his national rites, admitted with implicit faith the different religions of the earth. Fear, gratitude, and curiosity, a dream or an omen, a singular disorder, or a distant journey, perpetually disposed him to multiply the articles of his belief, and to enlarge the list of his protectors. The thin texture of the pagan mythology was interwoven with various but not discordant materials. As soon as it was allowed that sages and heroes, who had lived or who had died for the benefit of their country, were exalted to a state of power and immortality, it was universally confessed that they deserved, if not the adoration, at least the reverence of all mankind. The deities of a thousand groves and a thousand streams possessed in peace their local and respective influence; nor could the Roman who deprecated the wrath of the Tiber deride the Egyptian who presented his offering to the beneficent genius of the Nile. The visible powers of Nature, the planets, and the elements, were the same throughout the universe. The invisible governors of the moral world were inevitably cast in a similar mold of fiction and allegory. Every virtue, and even vice, acquired its divine representative; every art and profession its patron, whose attributes in the most distant ages and countries were uniformly derived from the character of their peculiar votaries. A republic of gods of such opposite tempers and interests required, in every system, the moderating hand of a supreme magistrate, who, by the progress of knowledge and of flattery, was gradually invested with the sublime perfections of an Eternal Parent and an Omnipotent Monarch. Such was the mild spirit of antiquity, that the nations were less attentive to the difference than to the resemblance of their religious worship. The Greek, the Roman, and the Barbarian, as they met before their respective altars, easily persuaded themselves that, under various names and with various ceremonies, they adored the same deities. The elegant mythology of Homer gave a beautiful and almost a regular form to the polytheism of the ancient world.

The philosophers of Greece deduced their morals from the nature of man rather than from that of God. They meditated, however, on the Divine Nature as a very curious and important speculation, and in the profound inquiry they displayed the strength and weakness of the human understanding. Of the four most celebrated schools, the Stoics and the Platonists endeavored to reconcile the jarring interests of reason and piety. They have left us the most sublime proofs of the existence and perfections of the first cause; but, as it was impossible for them to conceive the creation of matter, the workman in the Stoic philosophy was not sufficiently distinguished from the work; whilst, on the contrary, the spiritual God of Plato and his disciples resembled an idea rather than a substance. The opinions of the Academics and Epicureans were of a less religious cast; but, whilst the modest science of the former induced them to doubt, the positive ignorance of the latter urged them to deny, the providence of a Supreme Ruler. The spirit of inquiry, prompted by emulation and supported by freedom, had divided the public teachers of philosophy into a variety of contending sects; but the ingenuous youth, who from every part resorted to Athens and the other seats of learning in the Roman empire, were alike instructed in every school to reject and despise the religion of the multitude. How, indeed, was it possible that a philosopher should accept as divine truths the idle tales of the poets, and the incoherent traditions of antiquity; or that he should adore, as gods, those imperfect beings whom he must have despised, as men! Against such unworthy adversaries, Cicero condescended to employ the arms of reason and eloquence; but the satire of Lucian was a much more adequate as well as efficacious weapon. We may be well assured that a writer conversant with the world would never have ventured to expose the gods of his country to public ridicule, had they not already been the objects of secret contempt among the polished and enlightened orders of society.

Notwithstanding the fashionable irreligion which prevailed in the age of the Antonines, both the interests of the priests and the credulity of the people were sufficiently respected. In their writings and conversation the philosophers of antiquity asserted the independent dignity of reason; but they resigned their actions to the commands of law and of custom. Viewing with a smile of pity and indulgence the various errors of the vulgar, they diligently practised the ceremonies of their fathers, devoutly frequented the temples of the gods; and, sometimes condescending to act a part on the theatre of superstition, they concealed the sentiments of an Atheist under the sacerdotal robes. Reasoners of such a temper were scarcely inclined to wrangle about their respective modes of faith or of worship. It was indifferent to them what shape the folly of the multitude might choose to assume; and they approached, with the same inward contempt and the same external reverence, the altars of the Libyan, the Olympian, or the Capitoline Jupiter.

It is not easy to conceive from what motives a spirit of persecution could introduce itself into the Roman councils. The magistrates could not be actuated by a blind though honest bigotry, since the magistrates were themselves philosophers; and the schools of Athens had given laws to the senate. They could not be impelled by ambition or avarice, as the temporal and ecclesiastical powers were united in the same hands. The pontiffs were chosen among the most illustrious of the senators; and the office of Supreme Pontiff was constantly exercised by the emperors themselves. They knew and valued the advantages of religion, as it is connected with civil government. They encouraged the public festivals which humanize the manners of the people. They managed the arts of divination as a convenient instrument of policy; and they respected, as the firmest bond of society, the useful persuasion that, either in this or in a future life, the crime of perjury is most assuredly punished by the avenging gods. But, whilst they acknowledged the general advantages of religion, they were convinced that the various modes of worship contributed alike to the same salutary purposes; and that, in every country, the form of superstition which had received the sanction of time and experience was the best adapted to the climate and to its inhabitants. Avarice and taste very frequently despoiled the vanquished nations of the elegant statues of their gods and the rich ornaments of their temples; but, in the exercise of the religion which they derived from their ancestors, they uniformly experienced the indulgence, and even protection, of the Roman conquerors. The province of Gaul seems, and indeed only seems, an exception to this universal toleration. Under the specious pretext of abolishing human sacrifices, the emperors Tiberius and Claudius suppressed the dangerous power of the Druids; but the priests themselves, their gods, and their altars, subsisted in peaceful obscurity till the final destruction of Paganism.

Rome, the capital of a great monarchy, was incessantly filled with subjects and strangers from every part of the world, who all introduced and enjoyed the favorite superstitions of their native country. Every city in the empire was justified in maintaining the purity of its ancient ceremonies; and the Roman senate, using the common privilege, sometimes interposed to check this inundation of foreign rites. The Egyptian superstition, of all the most contemptible and abject, was frequently prohibited; the temples of Serapis and Isis demolished, and their worshippers banished from Rome and Italy. But the zeal of fanaticism prevailed over the cold and feeble efforts of policy. The exiles returned, the proselytes multiplied, the temples were restored with increasing splendor, and Isis and Serapis at length assumed their place among the Roman deities. Nor was this indulgence a departure from the old maxims of government. In the purest ages of the commonwealth, Cybele and Aesculapius had been invited by solemn embassies; and it was customary to tempt the protectors of besieged cities by the promise of more distinguished honors than they possessed in their native country. Rome gradually became the common temple of her subjects; and the freedom of the city was bestowed on all the gods of mankind.

The narrow policy of preserving without any foreign mixture the pure blood of the ancient citizens, had checked the fortune, and hastened the ruin, of Athens and Sparta. The aspiring genius of Rome sacrificed vanity to ambition, and deemed it more prudent, as well as honorable, to adopt virtue and merit for her own wheresoever they were found, among slaves or strangers, enemies or barbarians. During the most flourishing era of the Athenian commonwealth the number of citizens gradually decreased from about thirty to twenty-one thousand. If, on the contrary, we study the growth of the Roman republic, we may discover that, notwithstanding the incessant demands of wars and colonies, the citizens, who, in the first census of Servius Tullius, amounted to no more than eighty-three thousand, were multiplied, before the commencement of the social war, to the number of four hundred and sixty-three thousand men able to bear arms in the service of their country. When the allies of Rome claimed an equal share of honors and privileges, the senate indeed preferred the chance of arms to an ignominious concession. The Samnites and the Lucanians paid the severe penalty of their rashness; but the rest of the Italian states, as they successively returned to their duty, were admitted into the bosom of the republic, and soon contributed to the ruin of public freedom. Under a democratical government the citizens exercise the powers of sovereignty; and those powers will be first abused, and afterwards lost, if they are committed to an unwieldy multitude. But, when the popular assemblies had been suppressed by the administration of the emperors, the conquerors were distinguished from the vanquished nations only as the first and most honorable order of subjects; and their increase, however rapid, was no longer exposed to the same dangers. Yet the wisest princes who adopted the maxims of Augustus guarded with the strictest care the dignity of the Roman name, and diffused the freedom of the city with a prudent liberality.

Till the privileges of Romans had been progressively extended to all the inhabitants of the empire, an important distinction was preserved between Italy and the provinces. The former was esteemed the center of public unity, and the firm basis of the constitution. Italy claimed the birth, or at least the residence, of the emperors and the senate. The estates of the Italians were exempt from taxes, their persons from the arbitrary jurisdiction of governors. Their municipal corporations, formed after the perfect model of the capital, were intrusted, under the immediate eye of the supreme power, with the execution of the laws. From the foot of the Alps to the extremity of Calabria, all the natives of Italy were born citizens of Rome. Their partial distinctions were obliterated, and they insensibly coalesced into one great nation, united by language, manners, and civil institutions, and equal to the weight of a powerful empire. The republic gloried in her generous policy, and was frequently rewarded by the merit and services of her adopted sons. Had she always confined the distinction of Romans to the ancient families within the walls of the city, that immortal name would have been deprived of some of its noblest ornaments. Virgil was a native of Mantua; Horace was inclined to doubt whether he should call himself an Apulian or a Lucanian; it was in Padua that an historian was found worthy to record the majestic series of Roman victories. The patriot family of the Catos emerged from Tusculum; and the little town of Arpinum claimed the double honor of producing Marius and Cicero, the former of whom deserved, after Romulus and

Camillus, to be styled the Third Founder of Rome; and the latter, after saving his country from the designs of Catiline, enabled her to contend with Athens for the palm of eloquence.

The provinces of the empire (as they have been described in the preceding chapter) were destitute of any public force or constitutional freedom. In Etruria, in Greece, and in Gaul, it was the first care of the senate to dissolve those dangerous confederacies which taught mankind that, as the Roman arms prevailed by division, they might be resisted by union. Those princes whom the ostentation of gratitude or generosity permitted for a while to hold a precarious scepter were dismissed from their thrones, as soon as they had performed their appointed task of fashioning to the yoke the vanquished nations. The free states and cities which had embraced the cause of Rome were rewarded with a nominal alliance, and insensibly sunk into real servitude. The public authority was everywhere exercised by the ministers of the senate and of the emperors, and that authority was absolute and without control. But the same salutary maxims of government, which had secured the peace and obedience of Italy, were extended to the most distant conquests. A nation of Romans was gradually formed in the provinces, by the double expedient of introducing colonies, and of admitting the most faithful and deserving of the provincials to the freedom of Rome.

"Wheresoever the Roman conquers, he inhabits," is a very just observation of Seneca, confirmed by history and experience. The natives of Italy, allured by pleasure or by interest, hastened to enjoy the advantages of victory; and we may remark that, about forty years after the reduction of Asia, eighty thousand Romans were massacred in one day by the cruel orders of Mithridates. These voluntary exiles were engaged for the most part in the occupations of commerce, agriculture, and the farm of the revenue. But after the legions were rendered permanent by the emperors, the provinces were peopled by a race of sol-

diers; and the veterans, whether they received the reward of
their service in land or in money, usually settled with their
families in the country where they had honorably spent their
youth. Throughout the empire, but more particularly in the
western parts, the most fertile districts and the most convenient
situations were reserved for the establishment of colonies; some
of which were of a civil and others of a military nature. In their
manners and internal policy, the colonies formed a perfect
representation of their great parent; and as they were soon en-
deared to the natives by the ties of friendship and alliance, they
effectually diffused a reverence for the Roman name, and a desire which was seldom disappointed of sharing, in due time, its
honors and advantages. The municipal cities insensibly equalled
the rank and splendor of the colonies; and in the reign of
Hadrian it was disputed which was the preferable condition, of
those societies which had issued from, or those which had been
received into, the bosom of Rome. The right of Latium, at it
was called, conferred on the cities to which it had been granted
a more partial favor. The magistrates only, at the expiration of
their office, assumed the quality of Roman citizens; but as those
offices were annual, in a few years they circulated round the
principal families. Those of the provincials who were permitted
to bear arms in the legions; those who exercised any civil employment; all, in a word, who performed any public service, or
displayed any personal talents, were rewarded with a present,
whose value was continually diminished by the increasing
liberality of the emperors. Yet even in the age of the Antonines,
when the freedom of the city had been bestowed on the greater
number of their subjects, it was still accompanied with very
solid advantages. The bulk of the people acquired, with that
title, the benefit of the Roman laws, particularly in the interesting articles of marriage, testaments, and inheritances; and
the road of fortune was open to those whose pretensions were
seconded by favor or merit. The grandsons of the Gauls who

had besieged Julius Caesar in Alesia commanded legions, governed provinces, and were admitted into the senate of Rome. Their ambition, instead of disturbing the tranquillity of the state, was intimately connected with its safety and greatness.

So sensible were the Romans of the influence of language over national manners, that it was their most serious care to extend, with the progress of arms, the use of the Latin tongue. The ancient dialects of Italy, the Sabine, the Etruscan and the Venetian, sunk into oblivion; but in the provinces, the east was less docile than the west to the voice of its victorious preceptors. This obvious difference marked the two portions of the empire with a distinction of colors, which, though it was in some degree concealed during the meridian splendor of prosperity, became gradually more visible as the shades of night descended upon the Roman world. The western countries were civilized by the same hands which subdued them. As soon as the barbarians were reconciled to obedience, their minds were opened to any new impressions to knowledge and politeness. The language of Virgil and Cicero, though with some inevitable mixture of corruption, was so universally adopted in Africa, Spain, Gaul, Britain, and Pannonia, that the faint traces of the Punic or Celtic idioms were preserved only in the mountains, or among the peasants. Education and study insensibly inspired the natives of those countries with the sentiments of Romans; and Italy gave fashions, as well as laws, to her Latin provincials. They solicited with more ardor, and obtained with more facility, the freedom and honors of the state; supported the national dignity in letters and in arms; and, at length, in the person of Trajan, produced an emperor whom the Scipios would not have disowned for their countryman. The situation of the Greeks was very different from that of the barbarians. The former had been long since civilized and corrupted. They had too much taste to relinquish their language, and too much vanity to adopt any foreign institutions. Still preserving the prejudices, after they had lost the virtues, of their ancestors, they affected to despise the unpolished manners of the Roman conquerors, whilst they were compelled to respect their superior wisdom and power. Nor was the influence of the Grecian lànguage and sentiments confined to the narrow limits of that once celebrated country. Their empire, by the progress of colonies and conquest, had been diffused from the Hadriatic to the Euphrates and the Nile. Asia was covered with Greek cities, and the long reign of the Macedonian kings had introduced a silent revolution into Syria and Egypt. In their pompous courts those princes united the elegance of Athens with the luxury of the East, and the example of the court was imitated, at an humble distance, by the higher ranks of their subjects. Such was the general division of the Roman empire into the Latin and Greek languages. To these we may add a third distinction for the body of natives in Syria, and especially in Egypt. The use of their ancient dialects, by secluding them from the commerce of mankind, checked the improvement of those barbarians. The slothful effeminacy of the former exposed them to the contempt, the sullen ferociousness of the latter excited the aversion, of the conquerors. Those nations had submitted to the Roman power, but they seldom desired or deserved the freedom of the city; and it was remarked that more than two hundred and thirty years elapsed after the ruin of the Ptolemies, before an Egyptian was admitted into the senate of Rome.

It is a just though trite observation, that victorious Rome was herself subdued by the arts of Greece. Those immortal writers who still command the admiration of modern Europe soon became the favorite object of study and imitation in Italy and the western provinces. But the elegant amusements of the Romans were not suffered to interfere with their sound maxims of policy. Whilst they acknowledged the charms of the Greek, they asserted the dignity of the Latin, tongue, and the exclusive use of the latter was inflexibly maintained in the administration of civil as well as military government. The two languages exercised at the same time their separate jurisdiction throughout the empire: the former, as the natural idiom of science; the latter, as the legal dialect of public transactions. Those who united letters with business were equally conversant with both; and it was almost impossible, in any province, to find a Roman subject, of a liberal education, who was at once a stranger to the Greek and to the Latin language.

It was by such institutions that the nations of the empire insensibly melted away into the Roman name and people. But there still remained, in the center of every province and of every family, an unhappy condition of men who endured the weight, without sharing the benefits, of society. In the free states of antiquity the domestic slaves were exposed to the wanton rigor of despotism. The perfect settlement of the Roman empire was preceded by ages of violence and rapine. The slaves consisted, for the most part, of barbarian captives, taken in thousands by the chance of war, purchased at a vile price, accustomed to a life of independence, and impatient to break and to revenge their fetters. Against such internal enemies, whose desperate insurrections had more than once reduced the republic to the brink of destruction, the most severe regulations and the most cruel treatment seemed almost justified by the great law of self-preservation. But when the principal nations of Europe, Asia, and Africa were united under the laws of one sovereign, the source of foreign supplies flowed with much less abundance, and the Romans were reduced to the milder but more tedious method of propagation. In their numerous families, and particularly in their country estates, they encouraged the marriage of their slaves. The sentiments of nature, the habits of education, and the possession of a dependent species of property, contributed to alleviate the hardships of servitude. The existence of a slave became an object of greater value, and though his happiness still depended on the temper and circumstances of

the master, the humanity of the latter, instead of being restrained by fear, was encouraged by the sense of his own interest.
The progress of manners was accelerated by the virtue or policy
of the emperors; and by the edicts of Hadrian and the Antonines the protection of the laws was extended to the most abject
part of mankind. The jurisdiction of life and death over the
slaves, a power long exercised and often abused, was taken out
of private hands, and reserved to the magistrates alone. The
subterraneous prisons were abolished; and, upon a just complaint of intolerable treatment, the injured slave obtained either
his deliverance or a less cruel master.

Hope, the best comfort of our imperfect condition, was not
denied to the Roman slave; and, if he had any opportunity of
making himself either useful or agreeable, he might very naturally expect that the diligence and fidelity of a few years would
be rewarded with the inestimable gift of freedom. The benev-
olence of the master was so frequently prompted by the meaner
suggestions of vanity and avarice, that the laws found it more
necessary to restrain than to encourage a profuse and undis-
tinguishing liberality, which might degenerate into a very
dangerous abuse. It was a maxim of ancient jurisprudence, that
a slave had not any country of his own; he acquired with his
liberty an admission into the political society of which his
patron was a member. The consequences of this maxim would
have prostituted the privileges of the Roman city to a mean
and promiscuous multitude. Some seasonable exceptions were
therefore provided; and the honorable distinction was confined
to such slaves only as, for just causes, and with the approbation
of the magistrate, should receive a solemn and legal manu-
mission. Even these chosen freedmen obtained no more than
the private rights of citizens, and were rigorously excluded from
civil or military honors. Whatever might be the merit of fortune of their sons, *they* likewise were esteemed unworthy of a
seat in the senate; nor were the traces of a servile origin allowed

to be completely obliterated until the third or fourth generation. Without destroying the distinction of ranks, a distant
prospect of freedom and honors was presented, even to those
whom pride and prejudice almost disdained to number among
the human species.

It was once proposed to discriminate the slaves by a peculiar
habit, but it was justly apprehended that there might be some
danger in acquainting them with their own numbers. Without
interpreting, in their utmost strictness, the liberal appellations
of legions and myriads, we may venture to pronounce that the
proportion of slaves, who were valued as property, was more
considerable than that of servants, who can be computed only
as an expense. The youths of a promising genius were instructed
in the arts and sciences, and their price was ascertained by the
degree of their skill and talents. Almost every profession, either
liberal or mechanical, might be found in the household of an
opulent senator. The ministers of pomp and sensuality were
multiplied beyond the conception of modern luxury. It was
more for the interest of the merchant or manufacturer to pur-
chase than to hire his workmen; and in the country slaves were
employed as the cheapest and most laborious instruments of
agriculture. To confirm the general observation, and to display
the multitude of slaves, we might allege a variety of particular
instances. It was discovered, on a very melancholy occasion, that
four hundred slaves were maintained in a single palace of Rome.
The same number of four hundred belonged to an estate, which
an African widow, of a very private condition, resigned to her
son, whilst she reserved for herself a much larger share of her
property. A freedman, under the reign of Augustus, though his
fortune had suffered great losses in the civil wars, left behind
him three thousand six hundred yoke of oxen, two hundred and
fifty thousand head of smaller cattle, and, what was almost included in the description of cattle, four thousand one hundred
and sixteen slaves.

The number of subjects who acknowledged the laws of Rome, of citizens, of provincials, and of slaves, cannot now be fixed with such a degree of accuracy as the importance of the object would deserve. We are informed that, when the emperor Claudius exercised the office of censor, he took an account of six millions nine hundred and forty-five thousand Roman citizens, who with the proportion of women and children, must have amounted to about twenty millions of souls. The multitude of subjects of an inferior rank was uncertain and fluctuating. But, after weighing with attention every circumstance which could influence the balance, it seems probable that there existed, in the time of Claudius, about twice as many provincials as there were citizens, of either sex and of every age; and that the slaves were at least equal in number to the free inhabitants of the Roman world. The total amount of this imperfect calculation would rise to about one hundred and twenty millions of persons: a degree of population which possibly exceeds that of modern Europe, and forms the most numerous society that has ever been united under the same system of government.

Domestic peace and union were the natural consequences of the moderate and comprehensive policy embraced by the Romans. If we turn our eyes towards the monarchies of Asia, we shall behold despotism in the center and weakness in the extremities; the collection of the revenue, or the administration of justice, enforced by the presence of an army; hostile barbarians, established in the heart of the country, hereditary satraps usurping the dominion of the provinces and subjects, inclined to rebellion, though incapable of freedom. But the obedience of the Roman world was uniform, voluntary, and permanent. The vanquished nations, blended into one great people, resigned the hope, nay even the wish, of resuming their independence, and scarcely considered their own existence as distinct from the existence of Rome. The established author-

ity of the emperors pervaded without an effort the wide extent
of their dominions, and was exercised with the same facility
on the banks of the Thames, or of the Nile, as on those of the
Tiber. The legions were destined to serve against the public
enemy, and the civil magistrate seldom required the aid of a
military force. In this state of general security, the leisure as
well as opulence both of the prince and people were devoted
to improve and to adorn the Roman empire. . . .

PART THREE:
SUNSET IN THE WEST

Woe unto thee, Rome, oppressed and trodden under foot by so many nations! Thou art taken captive by the Saxon king [Otto the Great], thy people are put to the sword, thy strength is brought to naught. Thy gold and thy silver are carried away in their purses. The mother thou wast—a daughter thou hast become. What thou hadst, thou hast lost. Thou art despoiled of thy former strength. . . . Formerly, glorying in thy power, thou hast triumphed over nations, hast cast the world into the dust, hast strangled the kings of the earth. Thou hast grasped the scepter and wielded great power. Now art thou plundered and utterly despoiled by the Saxon king. As some wise men say, and as it will be found written in thy histories, thou didst once fight with foreign nations and conquer them from north to south. Now the people of Gaul have encamped in the midst of thee. Thou wast too beautiful.

Benedict of St. Andrea, about 968 (trans. Robinson)

ST. JEROME

Himself the brilliant product of a classical education, Jerome was as strongly affected as any pagan by the calamities which beset Rome in the age of the Germanic invasions.

On both Jerome and Augustine see E. K. Rand, Founders of the Middle Ages (Cambridge, Mass., 1929; reprinted, Dover paperback). On the classical culture of Jerome, which is evident in his ready citation of Roman poets: Harald Hagendahl, Latin Fathers and the Classics, Acta Universitatis Gothoburgensis, LXIV, 2 (1958).

There is a concise account of "The Empire and its Invaders" in M. L. W. Laistner, Thought and Letters in Western Europe, A.D. 500 to 900 (New York, 1931), pp. 1-9. Like other historians, Laistner observed that "there was nothing cataclysmic about the Germanic invasions. The decline and fall of the Western Empire was a gradual process lasting two centuries. . . . All, or nearly all, the invaders had become to some extent familiar with Roman institutions and Roman culture. Many of them alternated between hostility to Rome and alliance with her as foederati. And, even when they were her political enemies and invaded her territories, they were filled with awe at her name and respected her venerable civilization" (p. 9). And in reading Jerome we do well to heed Laistner's warning to "be on our guard against the exaggerations of the contemporary Latin writers." See also J. R. Palanque, "St. Jerome and the Barbarians," in A Monument to Saint Jerome (New York, 1952), pp. 171-200.

From The Principal Works of St. Jerome, trans. W. F. Fremantle, with the assistance of G. Lewis and W. G. Martley. A Select Library of Nicene and Post-Nicene Fathers of the Christian Church, Second Series, Volume VI (New York: Christian Literature Company, 1893).

MISERIES AND CALAMITIES
(Letter LX, 15-16)

. . . BUT why do I try to heal a sorrow which has already, I suppose, been assuaged by time and reason?[1] Why do I not rather unfold to you—they are not far to seek—the miseries of our rulers and the calamities of our time? He who has lost the light of life is not so much to be pitied as he is to be congratulated who has escaped from such great evils. Constantius, the patron of the Arian heresy, was hurrying to do battle with his enemy when he died at the village of Mopsus and to his great vexation left the empire to his foe.[2] Julian, the betrayer of his own soul, the murderer of a Christian army, felt in Media the hand of the Christ whom he had previously denied in Gaul. Desiring to annex new territories to Rome, he did but lose annexations previously made. Jovian had but just tasted the sweets of sovereignty when a coal-fire suffocated him: a good instance of the transitoriness of human power. Valentinian died of a broken blood vessel, the land of his birth laid waste, and his country unavenged. His brother Valens defeated in Thrace by the Goths, was buried where he died.[3] Gratian, betrayed by his army and refused admittance by the cities on his line of march, became the laughing-stock of his foe; and your walls, Lyons, still bear the marks of that bloody hand.[4] Valentinian was yet a youth—I may say, a mere boy—when, after flight and exile and the recovery of his power by bloodshed, he was put to death not far from the city which had witnessed his brother's end. And not only so but his lifeless body was gibbeted to do him shame. What shall I say of Procopius, of Maximus, of Eugenius,[5] who while they held sovereign sway were a terror to the nations, yet stood one and all as prisoners in the presence of their conquerors, and—cruellest wound of all to the great and powerful—felt the pang of an ignominious slavery before they fell by the edge of the sword.

Some one may say: such is the lot of kings: "The lightning ever smites the mountain-tops."[6] I will come therefore to persons of private position, and in speaking of these I will not go farther back than the last two years. In fact I will content myself—omitting all others—with recounting the respective fates of three recent consulars. Abundantius is a beggared exile at Pityus. The head of Rufinus has been carried on a pike to Constantinople, and his severed hand has begged alms from door to door to shame his insatiable greed. Timasius, hurled suddenly from a position of the highest rank thinks it an escape that he is allowed to live in obscurity at Assa. I am describing not the misfortunes of an unhappy few but the thread upon which human fortunes as a whole depend. I shudder when I think of the catastrophes of our time. For twenty years and more the blood of Romans has been shed daily between Constantinople and the Julian Alps. Scythia, Thrace, Macedonia, Dardania, Dacia, Thessaly, Achaia, Epirus, Dalmatia, the Pannonias—each and all of these have been sacked and pillaged and plundered by Goths and Sarmatians, Quades and Alans, Huns and Vandals and Marchmen. How many of God's matrons and virgins, virtuous and noble ladies, have been made the sport of these brutes! Bishops have been made captive, priests and those in minor orders have been put to death. Churches have been overthrown, horses have been stalled by the altars of Christ, the relics of martyrs have been dug up.

> Mourning and fear abound on every side
> And death appears in countless shapes and forms.[7]

The Roman world is falling: yet we hold up our heads instead of bowing them. What courage, think you, have the Corinthians now, or the Athenians or the Lacedaemonians or the

Arcadians, or any of the Greeks over whom the barbarians bear sway? I have mentioned only a few cities, but these once the capitals of no mean states. The East, it is true, seemed to be safe from all such evils: and if men were panic-stricken here, it was only because of bad news from other parts. But lo! in the year just gone by the wolves (no longer of Arabia but of the whole North[8]) were let loose upon us from the remotest fastnesses of Caucasus and in a short time overran these great provinces. What a number of monasteries they captured! What many rivers they caused to run red with blood! They laid siege to Antioch and invested other cities on the Halys, the Cydnus, the Orontes, and the Euphrates. They carried off troops of captives. Arabia, Phenicia, Palestine and Egypt, in their terror fancied themselves already enslaved.

> Had I a hundred tongues, a hundred lips,
> A throat of iron and a chest of brass,
> I could not tell men's countless sufferings.[9]

And indeed it is not my purpose to write a history: I only wish to shed a few tears over your sorrows and mine. For the rest, to treat such themes as they deserve, Thucydides and Sallust would be as good as dumb.

---

[1] Jerome is writing (396) to his old friend, Heliodorus, Bishop of Altinum, to console him for the recent death of his nephew.
[2] Constantius died in 361; his enemy, Julian, in 363; Jovian in 364; and Valentinian in 375.
[3] After the battle of Hadrianople (378).
[4] Gratian died in 383 at the hand of Andragathius; his half-brother, Valentinian II (b. 371) was strangled at Vienne in 392 by Arbogast.
[5] Aspirants who were put to death—the first by Valens, the others by Theodosius (379-395).
[6] Horace, Carmina II, x, 11-12.
[7] Aeneid II, 368-369.
[8] The Huns have taken the place of the Chaldaeans of Habakkuk i, 8.
[9] Aeneid VI, 625-627.

FURTHER MISERIES
(Letter CXXIII, 16-17)

. . . I SHALL now say a few words of our present miseries. A
few of us have hitherto survived them, but this is due not to
anything we have done ourselves but to the mercy of the Lord.
Savage tribes in countless numbers have overrun all parts of
Gaul. The whole country between the Alps and the Pyrenees,
between the Rhine and the Ocean, has been laid waste by hordes
of Quadi, Vandals, Sarmatians, Alans, Gepids, Herules,
Saxons, Burgundians, Allemanni and—alas! for the common-
weal!—even Pannonians. For "Assur also is joined with them."[1]
The once noble city of Moguntiacum has been captured and
destroyed. In its church many thousands have been massacred.
The people of Vangium after standing a long siege have been
extirpated. The powerful city of Rheims, the Ambiani, the
Altrebatae, the Belgians on the skirts of the world, Tournay,
Spires, and Strasburg have fallen to Germany: while the provinces of Aquitaine and of the Nine Nations, of Lyons and of
Narbonne are with the exception of a few cities one universal
scene of destruction. And those which the sword spares without,
famine ravages within. I cannot speak without tears of Toulouse
which has been kept from falling hitherto by the merits of its
reverend bishop Exuperius. Even the Spains are on the brink of
ruin and tremble daily as they recall the invasion of the Cymry;
and, while others suffer misfortunes once in actual fact, they
suffer them continually in anticipation.

I say nothing of other places that I may not seem to despair
of God's mercy. All that is ours now from the Pontic Sea to the
Julian Alps in days gone by once ceased to be ours. For thirty
years the barbarians burst the barrier of the Danube and fought
in the heart of the Roman Empire. Long use dried our tears.

For all but a few old people had been born either in captivity or during a blockade, and consequently they did not miss a liberty which they had never known. Yet who will hereafter credit the fact or what histories will seriously discuss it, that Rome has to fight within her own borders not for glory but for bare life; and that she does not even fight but buys the right to exist by giving gold and sacrificing all her substance? This humiliation has been brought upon her not by the fault of her Emperors[2] who are both most religious men, but by the crime of a half-barbarian traitor who with our money has armed our foes against us. Of old the Roman Empire was branded with eternal shame because after ravaging the country and routing the Romans at the Allia, Brennus with his Gauls entered Rome itself. Nor could this ancient stain be wiped out until Gaul, the birth-place of the Gauls, and Gaulish Greece, wherein they had settled after triumphing over East and West, were subjugated to her sway. Even Hannibal who swept like a devastating storm from Spain into Italy, although he came within sight of the city, did not dare to lay siege to it. Even Pyrrhus was so completely bound by the spell of the Roman name that destroying everything that came in his way, he yet withdrew from its vicinity and, victor though he was, did not presume to gaze upon what he had learned to be the city of kings. Yet in return for such insults—not to say such haughty pride—as theirs which ended thus happily for Rome, one banished from all the world found death at last by poison in Bithynia; while the other returning to his native land was slain in his own dominions. The countries of both became tributary to the Roman people. But now, even if complete success attends our arms, we can wrest nothing from our vanquished foes but what we have already lost to them. The poet Lucan describing the power of the city in a glowing passage says: "If Rome be weak, where shall we look for strength?"[3] We may vary his words and say: "If Rome be lost, where shall we look for help?" or quote the language of Virgil:

> Had I a hundred tongues and throat of bronze
> The woes of captives I could not relate
> Or ev'n recount the names of all the slain.[4]

Even what I have said is fraught with danger both to me who say it and to all who hear it; for we are no longer free even to lament our fate, and are unwilling, nay, I may even say, afraid to weep for our sufferings. . . .

---

[1] Ps. 1xxxiii, 8. Jerome's letter dates from 409.
[2] Arcadius and Honorius. Stilicho had persuaded the senate to grant a subsidy to the Gothic king, Alaric. (Stilicho himself was of Germanic stock.)
[3] *Pharsalia* V, 274.
[4] *Aeneid* VI, 625-627.

AFTERMATH

(Commentary on Ezekiel: Preface to Book III)

WHO would believe that Rome, built up by the conquest of the whole world, had collapsed,[1] that the mother of nations had become also their tomb; that the shores of the whole East, of Egypt, or Africa, which once belonged to the imperial city, were filled with the hosts of her men-servants and maid-servants, that we should every day be receiving in this holy Bethlehem men and women who once were noble and abounding in every kind of wealth, but are now reduced to poverty? We cannot relieve these sufferers: all we can do is to sympathize with them, and unite our tears with theirs. The burden of this holy work was as much as we could carry; the sight of the wanderers, coming in crowds, caused us deep pain; and we therefore abandoned the exposition of Ezekiel, and almost all study, and were filled with a longing to turn the words of Scripture into action, and not to say holy things but to do them. Now, however, in response to your admonition, Eustochium, Christ's virgin, we resume the interrupted labor, and approach our third Book.

1 Alaric had sacked Rome in August of 410.

RUTILIUS NAMATIANUS

That Alaric's sack of Rome had not completely effaced the city's splendor is evident from the glowing tribute written six years later by Rutilius Namatianus, the last of the classical Latin poets.

Rutilius came from a prominent Gallo-Roman family; and before returning to his native land he had held high offices under the emperor Honorius (395-423). Like Jerome, he hated Stilicho, whom in a fierce invective (II, 41-62) he accuses of destroying "the mother of the world."

On Rutilius and his age see Samuel Dill, Roman Society in the Last Century of the Western Empire, 2nd. ed. (London, 1925); E. S. Duckett, Latin Writers of the Fifth Century (New York, 1930), pp. 35-44; and Charles Henry Coster, "Christianity and the Invasions: Two Sketches," Classical Journal 54 (1959), 145-159 (esp. 153-156).

Reprinted by permission of the publishers and The Loeb Classical Library from J. W. Duff and A. M. Duff, translators, Minor Latin Poets (Cambridge, Mass.: Harvard University Press).

ROME'S SWAN-SONG
(*De Reditu Suo* I, 1-164)

RATHER will you marvel, reader, that my quick return journey (to Gaul) can so soon renounce the blessings of the city of Romulus. What is too long for men who spend all time in venerating Rome? Nothing is ever too long that never fails to please. How greatly and how often can I count those blest who have deserved birth in that happy soil! Those highborn scions of Roman nobility crown their honorable birth with the lustre of the Capital! On no other land could the seeds of virtues have been more worthily let fall by heaven's assignment. Happy they too who, winning meeds next to the first, have enjoyed Latin homes! The Senate-house, though fenced with awe, yet stands open to foreign merit, nor deems those strangers who are fittingly its own. They share the power of their colleagues in the senatorial order, and possess part of the sacred Genius which they revere, even as from the ethereal pole to pole of the celestial vault we believe there abideth the council of the Deity Supreme. (18)

But 'tis my fortune that is plucked back from the well-loved land: the fields of Gaul summon home their native. Disfigured they are by wars immeasurably long, yet the less their charm, the more they earn pity. 'Tis a lighter crime to neglect our countrymen when at their ease: our common losses call for each man's loyalty. Our presence and our tears are what we owe to the ancestral home: service which grief has prompted ofttimes helps. 'Tis sin further to overlook the tedious tale of disasters which the delay of halting aid has multiplied: now is the time after cruel fires on ravaged farms to rebuild, if it be but shepherds' huts. Nay, if only the very springs could utter words, if

only our very trees could speak, they well might spur my laggard
pace with just complaints and give sails to my yearning wishes.
Now that the dear city slackens her embrace, my homeland
wins, and I can scarce feel patient with a journey deferred so
late. (36)

I have chosen the sea, since roads by land, if on the level,
are flooded by rivers; if on higher ground, are beset with rocks.
Since Tuscany and since the Aurelian highway, after suffering
the outrages of Goths with fire or sword, can no longer control
forests with homestead or river with bridge, it is better to en-
trust my sails to the wayward sea. Repeated kisses I imprint on
the gates I have to leave: unwillingly my feet cross the honored
threshold. In tears I beseech pardon (for my departure) and
offer a sacrifice of praise, so far as weeping allows the words to
run: (46)

"Listen, O fairest queen of thy world, Rome, welcomed amid
the starry skies, listen, thou mother of men and mother of gods,
thanks to thy temples we are not far from heaven: thee do we
chant, and shall, while destiny allows, for ever chant. None
can be safe if forgetful of thee. Sooner shall guilty oblivion
whelm the sun than the honor due to thee quit my heart: for
thy benefits extend as far as the sun's rays, where the circling
Ocean-flood bounds the world. For thee the very Sun-God who
holdeth all together doth revolve: his steeds that rise in thy
domains he puts in thy domains to rest. Thee Africa hath not
stayed with scorching sands, nor hath the Bear, armed with its
native cold, repulsed thee. As far as living nature hath stretched
towards the poles, so far hath earth opened a path for thy valor.
For nations far apart thou hast made a single fatherland; under
thy dominion captivity hath meant profit even for those who
knew not justice: and by offering to the vanquished a share in
thine own justice, thou hast made a city of what was erstwhile
a world. (66)

"As authors of our race we acknowledge Venus and Mars—

mother of the sons of Aeneas, father of the scions of Romulus: clemency in victory tempers armed strength: both names befit thy character: hence thy noble pleasure in war and in mercy: it vanquishes the dreaded foe and cherishes the vanquished. The goddess who found the olive-tree is worshipped, the deity too who discovered wine, and the youth who first drove the plough-share in the soil;[1] the healing art through the skill of the god Paeon won altars: Hercules by his renown was made divine: thou, too, who hast embraced the world in triumphs fraught with law, dost make all things live under a common covenant. Thee, O goddess, thee every nook of the Roman dominion celebrates, beneath a peaceful yoke holding necks unenslaved. The stars, which watch all things in their unceasing motion, never looked on a fairer empire. What like unto thy power did it fall to Assyrian arms to link in one? The Persians only sub-dued neighbors of their own. The mighty Parthian kings and Macedonian monarchs imposed laws on each other through varying changes. It was not that at thy birth thou hadst more souls and hands: but more prudence and more judgment were thine. By wars for justifiable cause and by peace imposed with-out arrogance thy renowned glory reached highest wealth. That thou reignest is less than that thou deservest to reign: thy deeds surpass thine exalted destiny. To review thy high honors amid crowded trophies were a task like endeavoring to reckon up the stars. The glittering temples dazzle the wandering eyes: I could well believe such are the dwelling-places of the very gods. What shall I say of streams suspended on airy arches,[2] where scarce the Rainbow-Goddess could raise her showery waters? You might rather call them mountains grown up to the sky: such a structure Greece would praise, as giant-wrought. Rivers diverted are lost sight of within thy walls: the lofty baths con-sume whole lakes. No less are thy dewy meads filled also with their own rivulets, and all thy walls are a-babble with springs from the soil. Hence a breath of coolness tempers the summer

air, and the crystal well relieves a harmless thirst. Nay, once a
sudden torrent of waters seething hot broke forth, when thine
enemy[3] trod the roads by the Capitol: had it lasted for ever,
mayhap I had deemed this mere chance; but it was to save thee
that it flowed; for it came only to vanish. Why speak of woods
enclosed amid thy panelled palaces, where native birds sport
with varied song? In the spring that is thine never does the year
fail in its mildness: baffled winter respects thy charms. (114)

"Raise, O Rome, the triumphal laurels which wreathe thy
locks, and refashion the hoary eld of thy hallowed head to
tresses fresh and fair. Golden let the diadem flash on thy tower-
crowned helmet; let forgetfulness of thy wrongs bury the
sadness of misfortune; let pain disregarded close and heal thy
wounds. Amidst failure it is thy way to hope for prosperity:
after the pattern of the heavens losses undergone enrich thee.
For flaming stars set only to renew their rising; thou seest the
moon wane to wax afresh. The Allia did not hinder Brennus'
penalty; the Samnite paid for a cruel treaty by slavery; after
many disasters, though defeated, thou didst put Pyrrhus to
flight; Hannibal himself was the mourner of his own successes.
Things which cannot be sunk rise again with greater energy,
sped higher in their rebound from lowest depths; and, as the
torch held downward regains fresh strength, so from lowly
fortune thou dost soar more radiant aloft. Spread forth the laws
that are to last throughout the ages of Rome: alone thou needst
not dread the distaffs of the Fates, though with a thousand years
and sixteen decades o'erpast, thou hast besides a ninth year in
its course.[4] The span which doth remain is subject to no bounds,
so long as earth shall stand firm and heaven uphold the stars!
That same thing builds thee up which wrecks all other realms:
the law of thy new birth is the power to thrive upon thine
ills. (140)

"Come, then, let an impious race fall in sacrifice at last: let
the Goths in panic abase their forsworn necks. Let lands re-

duced to peace pay rich tribute and barbarian booty fill thy majestic lap. Evermore let the Rhineland plough for thee, for thee the Nile o'erflow; and let a teeming world give nurture to its nurse. Yea, let Africa proffer to thee her fertile harvests, rich in her own sun, but richer for thy showers. Meanwhile may granaries too arise to house the furrow-crops of Latium, and with the nectar of the West may sleek winepresses flow. Let Tiber's self, garlanded with triumphal reed, apply his waters to serve the needs of Romulus' race, and 'twixt his peaceful banks bear for thee down-stream the wealthy cargoes of the fields and up-stream those of the sea. (154)

"Outstretch, I pray, the level main lulled to rest 'neath Castor and his twin brother; be our Lady of Cythera the guide to smooth my watery path, if I found favor when I administered Quirinus' laws, if to the venerable senators I showed respect and from them asked advice; for that ne'er a crime unsheathed my magisterial sword[5] must be the people's, not the prefect's, boast. Whether 'tis granted to lay my life to rest in ancestral soil or whether thou shalt one day be restored to my eyes, blest shall my life be, lucky beyond all aspiration, if thou deign always to remember me." (164)

1 Athena (Minerva), Bacchus and Triptolemus.
2 That is, the aqueducts.
3 Titus Tatius and the Sabines.
4 The year 1169 of Rome = A.D. 416.
5 There was no capital punishment during his prefecture (414).

ST. AUGUSTINE

The City of God was begun as an answer to charges that Christianity had been responsible for Rome's woes, particularly its sack by the Goths; so Augustine's counter-attack naturally contains many harsh indictments of pagan Rome. But Augustine was a teacher of rhetoric before he became a Christian convert; and his deep appreciation of Roman literature, and of Rome's achievements, emerges at many points in the polemic.

See Albert C. Outler, "Augustine and the Transvaluation of the Classical Tradition," Classical Journal 54 (1959), 213-220; R. L. P. Milburn, Early Christian Interpretations of History (New York, 1954); and the last three essays in Theodor E. Mommsen, Medieval and Renaissance Studies, ed. Eugene F. Rice, Jr. (Ithaca, reissued 1966). There is a particularly relevant discussion of Augustine (and Orosius) in Charles Till Davis, Dante and the Idea of Rome (Oxford, 1957), pp. 40-73.

From The City of God, trans. Marcus Dods (Edinburgh: Clark, first impression, 1872; often reprinted).

THE ROMAN EXAMPLE
(*The City of God* V, 15-18)

NOW, therefore, with regard to those to whom God did not purpose to give eternal life with His holy angels in His own celestial city, to the society of which that true piety which does not render the service of religion, which the Greeks call *latreia*, to any save the true God conducts, if He had also withheld from them the terrestrial glory of that most excellent empire, a reward would not have been rendered to their good arts—that is, their virtues—by which they sought to attain so great glory. For as to those who seem to do some good that they may receive glory from men, the Lord also says, "Verily I say unto you, they have received their reward."[1] So also those despised their own private affairs for the sake of the republic, and for its treasury resisted avarice, consulted for the good of their country with a spirit of freedom, addicted neither to what their laws pronounced to be crime nor to lust. By all these acts, as by the true way, they pressed forward to honors, power, and glory; they were honored among almost all nations; they imposed the laws of their empire upon many nations; and at this day, both in literature and history, they are glorious among almost all nations. There is no reason why they should complain against the justice of the supreme and true God—"they have received their reward."

But the reward of the saints is far different, who even here endured reproaches for that city of God which is hateful to the lovers of this world. That city is eternal. There none are born, for none die. There is true and full felicity—not a goddess, but a gift of God. Thence we receive the pledge of faith, whilst on our pilgrimage we sigh for its beauty. There rises not the sun on the good and the evil, but the Sun of Righteousness protects the good alone. There no great industry shall be expended to enrich the public treasury by suffering privations at home, for there is the common treasury of truth. And, therefore, it was not only for the sake of recompensing the citizens of Rome that her empire and glory had been so signally extended, but also that the citizens of that eternal city, during their pilgrimage here, might diligently and soberly contemplate these examples, and see what a love they owe to the supernal country on account of life eternal, if the terrestrial country was so much beloved by its citizens on account of human glory.

For, as far as this life of mortals is concerned, which is spent and ended in a few days, what does it matter under whose government a dying man lives, if they who govern do not force him to impiety and iniquity? Did the Romans at all harm those nations, on whom, when subjugated, they imposed their laws, except in as far as that was accomplished with great slaughter in war? Now, had it been done with consent of the nations, it would have been done with greater success, but there would have been no glory of conquest, for neither did the Romans themselves live exempt from those laws which they imposed on others. Had this been done without Mars and Bellona, so that there should have been no place for victory, no one conquering where no one had fought, would not the condition of the Romans and of the other nations have been one and the same, especially if that had been done at once which afterwards was done most humanely and most acceptably, namely, the admission of all to the rights of Roman citizens who belonged to the Roman empire, and if that had been made the privilege of all which was formerly the privilege of a few, with this one condition, that the humbler class who had no lands of their own should live at the public expense—an alimentary impost, which would have been paid with a much better grace by them into the hands of good administrators of the republic, of which they

were members, by their own hearty consent, than it would
have been paid with had it to be extorted from them as conquered men? For I do not see what it makes for the safety,
good morals, and certainly not for the dignity, of men, that
some have conquered and others have been conquered, except
that it yields them that most insane pomp of human glory, in
which "they have received their reward," who burned with
excessive desire of it, and carried on most eager wars. For do not
their lands pay tribute? Have they any privilege of learning what
the others are not privileged to learn? Are there not many
senators in the other countries who do not even know Rome by
sight? Take away outward show, and what are all men after all
but men? But even though the perversity of the age should
permit that all the better men should be more highly honored
than others, neither thus should human honor be held at a
great price, for it is smoke which has no weight. But let us
avail ourselves even in these things of the kindness of God. Let
us consider how great things they despised, how great things
they endured, what lusts they subdued for the sake of human
glory, who merited that glory, as it were, in reward for such virtues; and let this be useful to us even in suppressing pride, so
that, as that city in which it has been promised us to reign as far
surpasses this one as heaven is distant from the earth, as eternal
life surpasses temporal joy, solid glory empty praise, or the society of angels the society of mortals, or the glory of Him who
made the sun and moon the light of the sun and moon, the citizens of so great a country may not seem to themselves to have
done anything very great, if, in order to obtain it, they have done
some good works or endured some evils, when those men for
this terrestrial country already obtained, did such great things,
suffered such great things. And especially are all these things to
be considered, because the remission of sins which collects
citizens to the celestial country has something in it to which a
shadowy resemblance is found in that asylum of Romulus,

whither escape from the punishment of all manner of crimes congregated that multitude with which the state was to be founded.

What great thing, therefore, is it for that eternal and celestial city to despise all the charms of this world, however pleasant, if for the sake of this terrestrial city Brutus could even put to death his son—a sacrifice which the heavenly city compels no one to make? But certainly it is more difficult to put to death one's sons, than to do what is required to be done for the heavenly country, even to distribute to the poor those things which were looked upon as things to be amassed and laid up for one's children, or to let them go, if there arise any temptation which compels us to do so, for the sake of faith and righteousness. For it is not earthly riches which make us or our sons happy; for they must either be lost by us in our lifetime, or be possessed when we are dead, by whom we know not, or perhaps by whom we would not. But it is God who makes us happy, who is the true riches of minds. But of Brutus, even the poet who celebrates his praises testifies that it was the occasion of unhappiness to him that he slew his son, for he says:

> And call his own rebellious seed
> For menaced liberty to bleed.
> Unhappy father! howsoe'er
> The deed be judged by after days.[2]

But in the following verse he consoles him in his unhappiness, saying: "His country's love shall all o'erbear." There are those two things, namely, liberty and the desire of human praise, which compelled the Romans to admirable deeds. If, therefore, for the liberty of dying men, and for the desire of human praise which is sought after by mortals, sons could be put to death by a father, what great thing is it, if, for the true liberty which has made us free from the dominion of sin, and death, and the devil —not through the desire of human praise, but through the earnest desire of freeing men, not from King Tarquin, but from demons and the prince of demons—we should, I do not say put to death our sons, but reckon among our sons Christ's poor ones? If, also, another Roman chief, surnamed Torquatus, slew his son, not because he fought against his country, but because, being challenged by an enemy, he through youthful impetuosity fought, though for his country, yet contrary to orders which he his father had given as general; and this he did, notwithstanding that his son was victorious, lest there should be more evil in the example of authority despised, than good in the glory of slaying an enemy;—if, I say, Torquatus acted thus, wherefore should they boast themselves, who, for the laws of a celestial country, despise all earthly good things, which are loved far less than sons? If Furius Camillus, who was condemned by those who envied him, notwithstanding that he had thrown off from the necks of his countrymen the yoke of their most bitter enemies, the Veientes, again delivered his ungrateful country from the Gauls, because he had no other in which he could have better opportunities for living a life of glory;—if Camillus did thus, why should he be extolled as having done some great thing, who, having it may be, suffered in the church at the hands of carnal enemies most grievous and dishonoring injury, has not betaken himself to heretical enemies, or himself raised some heresy against her, but has rather defended her, as far as he was able, from the most pernicious perversity of heretics, since there is not another church, I say not in which one can live a life of glory, but in which eternal life can be obtained? If Mucius, in order that peace might be made with King Porsenna, who was pressing the Romans with a most grievous war, when he did not succeed in slaying Porsenna, but slew another by mistake for him, reached forth his right hand and laid it on a red-hot altar, saying that many such as he saw him to be had conspired for his destruction, so that Porsenna, terrified at his daring, and at the thought of a conspiracy of such

as he, without any delay recalled all his warlike purposes, and
made peace;—if, I say, Mucius did this, who shall speak of his
meritorious claims to the kingdom of heaven, if for it he may
have given to the flames not one hand, but even his whole body,
and that not by his own spontaneous act, but because he was
persecuted by another? If Curtius, spurring on his steed, threw
himself all armed into a precipitous gulf, obeying the oracles of
their gods, which had commanded that the Romans should
throw into that gulf the best thing which they possessed, and
they could only understand thereby that, since they excelled
in men and arms, the gods had commanded that an armed man
should be cast headlong into that destruction;—if he did this,
shall we say that that man has done a great thing for the eternal
city who may have died by a like death, not, however, precipitat-
ing himself spontaneously into a gulf, but having suffered this
death at the hands of some enemy of his faith, more especially
when he has received from his Lord, who is also King of his
country, a more certain oracle, "Fear not them who kill the body,
but cannot kill the soul"?[3] If the Decii dedicated themselves to
death, consecrating themselves in a form of words, as it were,
that falling, and pacifying by their blood the wrath of the gods,
they might be the means of delivering the Roman army;—if
they did this, let not the holy martyrs carry themselves proudly,
as though they had done some meritorious thing for a share in
that country where are eternal life and felicity, if even to the
shedding of their blood, loving not only the brethren for whom
it was shed, but, according as had been commanded them, even
their enemies by whom it was being shed, they have vied with
one another in faith of love and love of faith. If Marcus Pul-
villus, when engaged in dedicating a temple to Jupiter, Juno,
and Minerva, received with such indifference the false intelligence which was brought to him of the death of his son, with
the intention of so agitating him that he should go away, and
thus the glory of dedicating the temple should fall to his col-

league;—if he received that intelligence with such indifference
that he even ordained that his son should be cast out unburied,
the love of glory having overcome in his heart the grief of be-
reavement, how shall any one affirm that he has done a great
thing for the preaching of the gospel, by which the citizens of
the heavenly city are delivered from divers errors, and gathered
together from divers wanderings, to whom his Lord has said,
when anxious about the burial of his father, "Follow me, and
let the dead bury their dead"?[4] Regulus, in order not to break
his oath, even with his most cruel enemies, returned to them
from Rome itself, because (as he is said to have replied to the
Romans when they wished to retain him) he could not have
the dignity of an honorable citizen at Rome after having been a
slave to the Africans, and the Carthaginians put him to death
with the utmost tortures, because he had spoken against them
in the senate. If Regulus acted thus, what tortures are not to
be despised for the sake of good faith toward that country to
whose beatitude faith itself leads? Or what will a man have
rendered to the Lord for all He has bestowed upon him, if, for
the faithfulness he owes to Him, he shall have suffered such
things as Regulus suffered at the hands of his most ruthless
enemies for the good faith which he owed to them? And how
shall a Christian dare vaunt himself of his voluntary poverty,
which he has chosen in order that during the pilgrimage of this
life he may walk the more disencumbered on the way which
leads to the country where the true riches are, even God Himself;—how, I say, shall he vaunt himself for this, when he hears
or reads that Lucius Valerius, who died when he was holding
the office of consul, was so poor that his funeral expenses were
paid with money collected by the people?—or when he hears
that Quintius Cincinnatus, who, possessing only four acres of
land, and cultivating them with his own hands, was taken from
the plough to be made dictator—an office more honorable even
than that of consul—and that, after having won great glory by

conquering the enemy, he preferred notwithstanding to continue in his poverty? Or how shall he boast of having done a great thing, who has not been prevailed upon by the offer of any reward of this world to renounce his connection with that heavenly and eternal country, when he hears that Fabricius could not be prevailed on to forsake the Roman city by the great gifts offered to him by Pyrrhus king of Epirus, who promised him the fourth part of his kingdom, but preferred to abide there in his poverty as a private individual? For if, when their republic—that is, the interest of the people, the interest of the country, the common interest—was most prosperous and wealthy, they themselves were so poor in their own houses, that one of them, who had already been twice a consul, was expelled from that senate of poor men by the censor, because he was discovered to possess ten pounds weight of silver-plate—since, I say, those very men by whose triumphs the public treasury was enriched were so poor, ought not all Christians, who make common property of their riches with a far nobler purpose, even that (according to what is written in the Acts of the Apostles) they may distribute to each one according to his need, and that no one may say that anything is his own, but that all things may be their common possession[5]—ought they not to understand that they should not vaunt themselves, because they do that to obtain the society of angels, when those men did well-nigh the same thing to preserve the glory of the Romans?

How could these, and whatever like things are found in the Roman history, have become so widely known, and have been proclaimed by so great a fame, had not the Roman empire, extending far and wide, been raised to its greatness by magnificent successes? Wherefore, through that empire, so extensive and of so long continuance, so illustrious and glorious also through the virtues of such great men, the reward which they sought was rendered to their earnest aspirations, and also examples are set before us, containing necessary admonition, in order that we may be stung with shame if we shall see that we have not held fast those virtues for the sake of the most glorious city of God, which are, in whatever way, resembled by those virtues which they held fast for the sake of the glory of a terrestrial city, and that, too, if we shall feel conscious that we have held them fast, we may not be lifted up with pride, because, as the apostle says, "The sufferings of the present time are not worthy to be compared to the glory which shall be revealed in us."[6] But so far as regards human and temporal glory, the lives of these ancient Romans were reckoned sufficiently worthy. Therefore, also, we see, in the light of that truth which, veiled in the Old Testament, is revealed in the New, namely, that it is not in view of terrestrial and temporal benefits, which divine providence grants promiscuously to good and evil, that God is to be worshipped, but in view of eternal life, everlasting gifts, and of the society of the heavenly city itself;—in the light of this truth we see that the Jews were most righteously given as a trophy to the glory of the Romans; for we see that these Romans, who rested on earthly glory, and sought to obtain it by virtues, such as they were, conquered those who, in their great depravity, slew and rejected the giver of true glory, and of the eternal city.

1 Matthew vi, 2.   4 Matthew viii, 22.
2 *Aeneid* VI, 820-822.   5 Acts ii, 45.
3 Matthew x, 28.   6 Romans viii, 18.

VALENTINIAN III

Even St. Jerome, for all his reverence toward Rome and the Church of Rome, had asserted the equality of all bishops; but during the pontificate of Leo the Great, the emperor issued an edict proclaiming the primacy of the bishop of Rome, a primacy strongly upheld in Leo's own writings. And not long afterwards (494), Pope Gelasius I felt important enough to advise the Eastern Emperor, Anastasius, about the papacy's superiority over any temporal power whatsoever. Sic transit gloria mundi. . . .

On Gelasius' influential views, see A. K. Ziegler, "Pope Gelasius I and his Teaching on the Relation of Church and State," The Catholic Historical Review XXVII (1942), 3-28. Later papal claims to temporal authority (against which Dante inveighed so passionately) were based in part on the so-called "Donation of Constantine," which, along with a fifteenth-century demonstration that it was a medieval forgery, may be read in The Treatise of Lorenzo Valla on the Donation of Constantine, ed. and trans. Christopher B. Coleman (New Haven, 1922).

From James Harvey Robinson, Readings in European History, Volume I (Ginn & Company, 1904). There are numerous other relevant texts in this fine volume.

THE SUPREMACY OF
THE BISHOP OF ROME
(Imperial edict of 445)

SINCE, then, the primacy of the Apostolic See is established by the merit of St. Peter (who is the chief among the bishops), by the majesty of the city of Rome, and finally by the authority of a holy council,[1] no one, without inexcusable presumption, may attempt anything against the authority of that see. Peace will be secured among the churches if every one recognize his ruler.

[After a reference to the independent action of certain prelates of Gaul, the edict continues.] Lest even a slight commotion should arise in the churches, or the religious order be disturbed, we herewith permanently decree that not only the bishops of Gaul, but those of the other provinces, shall attempt nothing counter to ancient custom without the authority of the venerable father [papa] of the Eternal City. Whatever shall be sanctioned by the authority of the Apostolic See shall be law to them and to every one else; so that if one of the bishops be summoned to the judgment of the Roman bishop and shall neglect to appear, he shall be forced by the moderator of his province to present himself. In all respects let the privileges be maintained which our deified predecessors have conferred upon the Roman church.

---

[1] The Council of Nicaea (325) had said nothing to indicate that the bishop of Rome held greater jurisdiction than other metropolitans; but the Council of Sardika eighteen years later decreed that a bishop who felt unjustly deposed by a synod might appeal to Rome.

JAMES VISCOUNT BRYCE

The western line of emperors, after ending in 476 with Romulus Augustulus, was renewed in 800 by Charlemagne (this was later called the "transference of the Empire from the Greeks to the Franks"). There followed an undistinguished succession of Carolingian and Italian emperors; then a more notable series was inaugurated in 962 by the coronation of a Saxon, Otto I (the Great).

The Holy Roman Empire did not come to an end until 1806, when Francis II announced his resignation of the crown; and Bryce's classic work was written some two generations later, during the years when national unification was finally being achieved in Italy and Germany, both of which countries have since entertained imperial dreams not entirely unrelated to their ancient and medieval past.

There is a brief recent assessment by Geoffrey Barraclough: The Mediaeval Empire; Idea and Reality (London, 1950). For a distinctly Roman focus in medieval history, see Giorgio Falco, The Holy Roman Republic: A Historic Profile of the Middle Ages, trans. K. V. Kent (London, 1964).

From James Viscount Bryce, The Holy Roman Empire, new edition (London: Macmillan, 1919 reissue). Reprinted with the permission of St. Martin's Press, Inc., Macmillan & Co., Ltd. and Macmillan Company of Canada.

ROME'S LEGACY TO
THE MIDDLE AGES
(*The Holy Roman Empire,* Ch. XXII:
Summary and Reflections)

AMONG the peoples around the Mediterranean, whose national feeling had died out, whose national faiths were extinct or had turned to superstition, whose thought and art had lost their force and freshness, there arose a giganatic military power, the power first of a city, then of an administrative system culminating in an irresponsible monarch, which pressing with equal weight on all its subjects, gave them a new imperial nationality, and became to them a religion as well as a government. When this system, weakened by internal decay, was at length beginning to dissolve, the tribes of the North came down, too rude to maintain the elaborate institutions they found subsisting, too few and scattered to introduce their own simpler institutions, and in the weltering confusion that followed, the idea of a civilized commonwealth would have perished, had not the association of a young and vigorous faith with the name and authority of Rome formed the foundation of a new unity, politically weak, but morally close and durable. Then the strong hand of the first Frankish Emperor raised the fallen image and bade the nations bow down to it once more. Under him it was for some brief space a sort of military theocracy; under his German successors the first of feudal kingdoms, the center of European chivalry. As feudalism wanes, the imperial office, as well as the imperial idea, was again transformed, and after promising for a time to become an hereditary

Hapsburg monarchy, it sank at last into the presidency, not more dignified than powerless, of an international league.

To the modern world, penetrated by a critical and practical spirit, a perpetuation under conditions so diverse of the same name and the same pretensions appears at first sight absurd, a phantom too vain to impress the most superstitious mind. Closer examination corrects such a notion. No power was ever based on foundations more sure and deep than those which Rome laid during three centuries of conquest and four of undisturbed dominion. If her empire had been an hereditary or local kingdom, it might have fallen with the extinction of the royal line, the overthrow of the tribe, the destruction of the city, to which it was attached. But it was not so limited. It was imperishable because it was universal; and when its power had ceased, it was remembered with awe and love by the races whose separate existence it had destroyed, because it had spared the weak while it smote down the strong; because it had granted equal rights to all, and closed against none of its subjects the path of honorable ambition. When the military power of the conquering city had departed, her sway over the world of thought began. By her the Greek theory of a commonwealth of mankind had been reduced to practice; the magic of her name remained, and she held a sway over the imagination which the passing of century after century scarcely reduced. She had gathered up and embodied in her literature and institutions all the ideas and all the practical results of ancient thought. Embracing and organizing and propagating the new religion, she made it seem her own. Her language, her theology, her laws, her architecture made their way where the eagles of war had never winged their flight, and with the spread of civilization have found new homes on the Ganges and the Mississippi.

Nor is such a claim of government prolonged under changed conditions by any means a singular phenomenon. Titles sum up the political history of nations, and are as often causes as effects: if significant to-day, how much more so in ages of ignorance when tradition was stronger than reason. Even in our time various pretensions have been put forward to represent the Empire of Rome, all of them without historical foundation, none of them without practical import. Austria clings to a name which seems to perpetuate the primacy held by Charles the Fifth in Europe, and was wont, while she held Lombardy, to justify her position there by invoking the feudal rights of Franconian and Swabian sovereigns. With no more legal right than a prince of Reuss or a grand duke of Mecklenburg might pretend to, she continued after the disappearance of the old Empire to use its arms and devices, and being almost the youngest of European monarchies, she became respected as the oldest and most conservative. Bonapartean France, as the self-appointed heir of the Carolingians, grasped for a time the scepter of the West, and under the ruler who fell in 1870 aspired to hold the balance of European politics, and be recognized as the leader and patron of the so-called "Latin races" on both sides of the Atlantic. Professing the creed of Constantinople, Russia claims the crown of the Eastern Caesars, and looks forward to the day when the capital which prophecy has promised for a thousand years will echo to the tramp of her armies. The doctrine of Panslavism, under an imperial head of the Orthodox Eastern Church has become a formidable engine of aggression in the hands of a mighty despotism and a growing race, naturally drawn to expand its frontiers toward the South. Another testimony to the enduring influence of old political combinations is supplied by the eagerness with which modern Hellas embraced the notion of gathering the peoples of South-Eastern Europe and Asia Minor that profess the Orthodox creed into a revived Empire of the East, with its capital on the Bosphorus. Nay, the intruding Ottoman himself, different in faith as well as in blood, long ago declared himself the representative of the Eastern Caesars, whose dominion he extinguished. Sultan Suleiman the Magnificent assumed the name of Emperor, and refused it to Charles the Fifth; his successors were once preceded through the streets of Constantinople by twelve officers, bearing straws aloft, a faint semblance of the consular fasces that had escorted a Quinctius or a Fabius through the Roman forum. Yet in no one of these cases was there that apparent legality of title which the shouts of the people and the benediction of the pontiff conveyed to Charles and Otto.

These examples, however, are minor parallels: the complement and illustration of the history of the Empire is to be found in that of the Holy See. The Papacy, whose spiritual power was itself the offspring of Rome's temporal dominion, evoked the phantom of her parent, used it, obeyed it, rebelled and overthrew it, in its old age once more drew it to her bosom, till in its downfall she heard the knell of the old order and saw the end of her own temporal power approaching.

Both Papacy and Empire rose in an age when the human spirit was prostrated before authority and tradition, when the exercise of private judgment was impossible to most and sinful to all. Those who believed the miracles recorded in the *Acta Sanctorum,* and did not question the Pseudo-Isidorian decretals, might well recognize as ordained of God the twofold authority of Rome, founded, as it seemed to be, on so many texts of Scripture, and confirmed by five centuries of undisputed possession.

Both sanctioned and satisfied the passion of the Middle Ages for Unity. Ferocity, violence, disorder, were the conspicuous evils of that time: hence all the aspirations of the good were for something which, breaking the force of passion and increasing the force of sympathy, should teach the stubborn wills to sacrifice themselves in the view of a common purpose. To those men, moreover, unable to rise above the sensuous, seeing with eyes unlike ours both the connection and the difference of the spiritual and the secular elements in life, the idea of the Visible Church was full of awful meaning. Solitary thought was helpless, and strove to lose itself in the aggregate, since it could not create for itself that which was universal. The schism that severed a man from the congregation of the faithful on earth was hardly less dreadful than the heresy which excluded him from the company of the blessed in heaven. He who kept not his appointed place in the ranks of the church militant had no right to swell the rejoicing anthems of the church triumphant. Here, as in so many other cases, the continued use of traditional language prevents men from seeing how great is the difference between their own times and those in which the phrases they repeat were first used, and used in full sincerity. Whether the world is better or worse for the change which has passed upon its feelings in these matters is another question: all that is necessary to note here is that the change is a profound and pervading one. Obedience, almost the first of mediaeval virtues, is now often spoken of as if it were fit only for slaves or fools. Instead of praising, men are wont to condemn the submission of the individual will, the surrender of the individual belief, to the will or the belief of the community. Some persons declare variety of belief to be a positive good. The great mass have little longing for a perfect unity of faith. They have no horror of schism. They cannot understand the fascination which the idea of one all-embracing, all-pervading church exercised upon their mediaeval forefathers. A life in the church, for the church, through the church; a life which she blessed in mass at morning and sent to peaceful rest by the vesper hymn; a life which she supported by the constantly recurring stimulus of the sacraments, relieving it by confession, purifying it by penance, admonishing it by the presentation of visible objects for contemplation and worship—this was the life which they of the Middle Ages conceived of as the rightful life for man; it was the actual life of many, the ideal of all. The unseen world was so unceasingly felt, that the barrier between the two seemed to disappear. The church was not merely the portal to heaven; it was heaven anticipated; it was already self-gathered and complete. In one sentence from a singular mediaeval document may be found a key to much which seems strangest to us in the feelings of the Middle Ages: "The church is dearer to God than heaven. For the church does not exist for the sake of heaven, but conversely, heaven for the sake of the church."

Again, both Empire and Papacy rested on opinion rather than on material force, and when the struggle which began in the eleventh century came, the Empire succumbed, because its rival's hold over the souls of men was firmer, more direct, enforced by penalties more terrible than the death of the body. The ecclesiastical host which Alexander III and Innocent IV led was animated by a loftier spirit and more wholly devoted to a single aim than the knights and nobles who followed the banner of the Swabian Caesars. Its allegiance was undivided; it comprehended the principles for which it fought. They trembled at even while they resisted the spiritual power.

Both sprang from what might seem to be the accident of name. The power of the great Latin patriarchs was a Form: the ghost, it has been said, of the older Empire, favored in its growth by circumstances, but really vital because capable of wonderful adaptation to the character and wants of the time. So too, though far less perfectly, was the Empire. Its Form was the tradition of the universal rule of Rome; it met the needs of successive centuries by civilizing barbarous peoples, by maintaining unity in confusion and disorganization, by controlling brute violence through the sanctions of a higher power, by being made the keystone of a gigantic feudal arch, by becoming in its old age the center of a European States-system. And its history, as it shews the power of ancient names and forms, shews also how hopeless is the attempt to preserve in life a system which arose out of ideas and under conditions that have passed away, how unreal such a perpetuation may be, and how it may deceive men, by preserving the shadow while it loses the substance. This perpetuation itself, what is it but the expression of the belief of mankind, a belief incessantly corrected yet never weakened, that their old institutions can continue to subsist unchanged, that what has served their fathers will do well enough for them, that it is possible to make a system once for all perfect and abide in it for ever thereafter? Of all political instincts this is perhaps the strongest; often useful, often abused, but never more natural or more fitting than when it led men who felt skill and knowledge slipping from their grasp to seek to save what they could from the wreck of an older and higher civilization. It was thus that both Papacy and Empire were maintained by generations who had no type of greatness and wisdom save that which they associated with the name of Rome. Though it never could have existed save as a prolongation, though it was and remained through the Middle Ages an anachronism, the Empire of the tenth century had changed profoundly from the Empire of the second. Much more was the Papacy, though it too hankered after the forms and titles of antiquity, a truly new creation. And in the same proportion as it was new, and represented the spirit not of a past age but of its own, was it a power stronger and more enduring than the Empire. More enduring, because more lately born, and so in fuller harmony with the ruling spirit and cogent needs of the time, stronger, because at the head of the great ecclesiastical body, in and through which, rather than through secular life, the intelligence and political activity of the Middle Ages sought their expression. The famous simile of Gregory the Seventh is that which best describes the Empire and the Popedom. They were indeed the "two lights in the firmament of the militant church," the lights which illumined and ruled

the world all through the Middle Ages. And as moonlight is to
sunlight, so was the Empire to the Papacy. The rays of the one
were borrowed, feeble, often interrupted: the other shone with
an unquenchable brilliance that was all her own.

If we analyze the Papacy and the Empire, we shall find that
each is old, and each is new. The remark is true in a sense of
all institutions, but it applies in a special sense to these two.
The Papacy was new in the doctrines and the spirit which it
drew from Scripture and Christian tradition. It was old in the
form of its government, for this was modelled on the heathen
autocracy, old also in the application of compulsive power to
matters of opinion and belief, than which nothing could be
more opposed to the teachings of Christ. The Empire was new
in so far as it was a German kingdom, built up on feudal principles; new also in all that it had imbibed from Christianity—
in the sense of its religious mission, and of faith as a bond to
unite mankind in one world-embracing state. It was old not
only in its name but in the effort to base its universal dominion
upon the imprescriptible rights of Rome, and in the autocratic
character which its adoption of the ancient Roman law as its
own had made it, at least in outward semblance, assume.

This distinction between its component elements may help
to supply an answer to the question which the student of its
history often puts to himself—"Was it Roman in anything but
name? and was that name anything better than a piece of fantastic antiquarianism?" A comparison might be drawn between
the Antonines of the second century and the Ottos of the
tenth which should shew nothing but unlikeness. What the
Empire was in the second century every student of the ancient
classics knows. In the tenth it was a feudal monarchy, resting
on a strong territorial oligarchy. Its chiefs were barbarians, the
sons of those who had destroyed Varus and baffled German-
icus, sometimes unable even to use the tongue of Rome. Its
powers, nominally wide, were limited by custom and the

strength of the great vassals. It could scarcely be said to have a governmental organization, whether judicial or administrative. It was consecrated to the defence, nay, it existed by virtue of the religion, which Trajan and Marcus had persecuted. Nevertheless, however strongly the contrast be stated points of resemblance will remain. The Roman idea of universal denationalization survived as an idea, and drew with it that of a certain equality among all free subjects. The world's highest dignity was for many centuries the only civil office to which any freeborn Christian was legally eligible. So too there survived the Roman conception of Law, written, settled, scientific law, as the foundation of social order, as the regulator of the relations of members of the community, as the form through which the state must act.

It may be added that there was among the Teutonic Emperors, when one compares them as a whole either with the East Roman monarchs or with the Muslim dynasties, a loftiness of spirit and a sense of duty to the realm they ruled which recalls the old Roman type. Trajan and Marcus might have found their true successors among the woods of Germany rather than in the palaces of Constantinople, where every office and name and custom had floated down from the court of Theodosius in a stream of unbroken legitimacy. The ceremonies of Henry the Seventh's coronation would have been strange indeed to Caius Julius Caesar Octavianus Augustus; yet they were better than the purple buskins of Byzantium: they had more Roman dignity and force than the fantastic forms with which a Palaeologus was installed! Of the Germanic Empire in later centuries the same cannot be said. It had lived on, when honor and nature bade it die: it had become what the empire of the Moguls had then become, and that of the Ottomans still later became, a curious relic of antiquity, on which the philosopher might muse, but from which the vigor of life and all power for good had long since departed. Institutions, however, should, like men, be judged by their prime.

In the beginning of the fourteenth century the thoughts and hopes of the purest and most earnest minds were directed to the ideal of a Universal Christian State, by which universal peace should be secured; a lofty ideal, and one never to be forgotten by mankind. In the centuries that followed, other aims, other ideals inspired the men who led the movement of the world, and five hundred years after Dante's time noble lives were being consecrated to the deliverance of every people from alien rule, and the establishment of each as a free self-governing community. This too was a high ideal, and a precious one, for it meant the extinction of many tyrannies and the drying up of many springs of race hatred. No wonder that the principle of nationalities was then advocated with honest devotion as the perfect form of political development. Yet finality cannot be claimed for this ideal, any more than for those that went before. If all other history did not bid us beware the habit of taking the problems and the conditions of our own age for those of all time, the warning which the history of the Empire gives might alone be warning enough. From the days of Augustus down to those of Charles the Fifth the whole civilized world believed in its existence as a part of the eternal fitness of things, and Christian theologians were not behind heathen poets in declaring that when it perished the world would perish with it. Yet the Empire vanished, and the world remained, and hardly noted the change.

The highest themes which can occupy the mind are, as Dante has said, those which most transcend the resources of human language. So in parting from a great subject the feeling arises that words fail to convey the ideas it suggests, and that however much may have been said, much must remain unsaid,

because incapable of expression. Here one is baffled partly by
the magnitude of the subject, for it is a vast one, which needs
to be studied as a whole, as an institution which through forty
generations of men preserves its name and its claims while its
relations to the world around it are constantly changing. But
another difficulty lies still deeper. It lies in grasping the essence
and spirit of the Holy Empire as it appeared to the saints and
poets of the Middle Ages, and in realizing all that it meant to
them. Formulas help us little: it is rather through imagination
than by logic or analysis that we may succeed in apprehending
the true significance of this strange creation of reverent tradition and mystical faith which filled the sky and scarcely
touched the earth. A like difficulty meets us when we think of
that other still more wonderful child of Rome and of tradition,
the Papacy. The Protestants of the seventeenth century, who
saw in it nothing but a gigantic upas-tree of fraud and superstition, planted and reared by the enemy of mankind, were hardly further from entering into the mystery of its being than
the complacent philosophers of the eighteenth century, who
explained in neat phrases the process of its growth, analyzed it
as a clever piece of mechanism, enumerating and measuring
the interests it appealed to. As there is a sense in which the
Papacy is above explanation, because it appeals to emotion, not
to reason, to faith, and not to sight, so of the Empire also may
this be said, not that it is impossible to discover the beliefs
which created and sustained it, but that the power and fascination of those beliefs cannot be adequately apprehended by men
whose minds have been differently trained, and whose imaginations are fired by different ideals. Something we should know
of it if we knew what were the thoughts of Julius Caesar when
he laid the foundations on which Augustus built; of Charles
the Great, when he reared anew the majestic pile; of Henry the
Third, when he consecrated the strength of his crown to the
purification of the Church; of Frederick "the Wonder of the

World," when he strove to avert the surely coming ruin. Something more succeeding generations will know, who may judge the Middle Ages more fairly then we, still influenced by a reaction against all that is mediaeval, can hope to do, and to whom it will be given to see and understand new forms of political life, whose nature we cannot conjecture. Seeing more than we do, they will also see some things less distinctly. The Empire which to us still looms largely on the horizon of the past, will to them sink lower and lower as they journey onwards into the future. But its importance in universal history it can never lose. For into it all the life of the ancient world was gathered: out of it all the life of the modern world arose.

PART FOUR: A CITY OF RUINS

The Niobe of nations! there she stands,
Childless and crownless, in her voiceless woe;
An empty urn within her withered hands,
Whose holy dust was scattered long ago;
The Scipios' tomb contains no ashes now;
The very sepulchres lie tenantless
Of their heroic dwellers: dost thou flow,
Old Tiber! through a marble wilderness?
Rise, with thy yellow waves, and mantle her distress.

The Goth, the Christian, Time, War, Flood, and Fire,
Have dealt upon the seven-hilled city's pride;
She saw her glories star by star expire,
And up the steep barbarian monarchs ride,
Where the car climbed the capitol; far and wide
Temple and tower went down, nor left a site:—
Chaos of ruins! who shall trace the void,
O'er the dim fragments cast a lunar light,
And say, "here was, or is," where all is doubly night?

Byron, *Childe Harold's Pilgrimage* IV, 79-80

WILLIAM OF MALMESBURY
and
HILDEBERT OF LAVARDIN

Perhaps the worst sack in the history of Rome was occasioned by the Investiture Controversy between Gregory VII and Henry IV. In March 1084 Henry entered Rome, was welcomed as a liberator by the rebellious people, and had himself crowned Holy Roman Emperor by an Anti-pope. But Gregory summoned to his aid Robert Guiscard, Duke of Apulia, who in May established his camp on the same spot where the Goths had encamped in 537. When Henry abandoned the Romans, the city was laid waste: "The desertion and desolation which five centuries later filled with wonder the soul of Joachim du Bellay date from this pillage by the Normans and Saracens who followed the standard of Robert Guiscard" (Raby, p. 267).

Such was the city of ruins which inspired Hildebert (1056-1133), when he visited Rome some two decades later, to compose his Roman Elegies. The first, on the pagan Rome of the past, was not long afterward quoted by the English chronicler, William of Malmesbury. The second is an answer by Christian Rome, ruler over souls, not bodies.

On Hildebert, "one of the most important literary figures of the Middle Ages," see F. J. E. Raby, A History of Christian-Latin Poetry, 2nd. ed. (Oxford, 1953), pp. 265-273. For a review of the many calamities suffered by Rome through the ages, see Rodolfo Lanciani, The Destruction of Ancient Rome (London, 1899).

From Chronicles of the Kings of England, with notes and illustrations by J. A. Giles (London: Bohn, 1847). Based on the translation of John Sharpe.

PAGAN AND CHRISTIAN ROME
(*Chronicle of the Kings of England* IV, 2)

. . . OF ROME, formerly the mistress of the globe, but which now, in comparison of its ancient state, appears a small town; and of the Romans, once "sovereign over all and the gowned nation,"[1] who are now the most fickle of men, bartering justice for gold, and dispensing with the canons for money; of this city and its inhabitants, I say, whatever I might attempt to write, has been anticipated by the verses of Hildebert, first, bishop of Mans, and afterwards archbishop of Tours. Which I insert, not to assume the honor acquired by another man's labor, but rather as a proof of a liberal mind, while not envying his fame, I give testimony to his charming poetry.

> Rome, still thy ruins grand beyond compare,
> Thy former greatness mournfully declare,
> Though time thy stately palaces around
> Hath strewed, and cast thy temples to the ground.
> Fall'n is the power, the power Araxes dire
> Regrets now gone, and dreaded when entire;
> Which arms and laws, and ev'n the gods on high
> Bade o'er the world assume the mastery;
> Which guilty Caesar rather had enjoyed
> Alone, than e'er a fostering hand employed.
> Which gave to foes, to vice, to friends its care,
> Subdued, restrained, or bade its kindness share
> This growing power the holy fathers reared,
> Where near the stream the fav'ring spot appeared
> From either pole, materials, artists meet,
> And rising walls their proper station greet;

Kings gave their treasures, fav'ring too was fate,
And arts and riches on the structure wait.
Fall'n is that city, whose proud fame to reach,
I merely say, "Rome was," there fails my speech.
Still neither time's decay, nor sword, nor fire,
Shall cause its beauty wholly to expire.
Human exertions raised that splendid Rome,
Which gods in vain shall strive to overcome.
Bid wealth, bid marble, and bid fate attend,
And watchful artists o'er the labor bend,
Still shall the matchless ruin art defy
The old to rival, or its loss supply.
Here gods themselves their sculptur'd forms admire,
And only to reflect those forms aspire;
Nature unable such like gods to form,
Left them to man's creative genius warm;
Life breathes within them, and the suppliant falls,
Not to the God, but statues in the walls.
City thrice blessed! were tyrants but away,
Or shame compelled them justice to obey.[2]

Are not these sufficient to point out in such a city, both the dignity of its former advantages, and the majesty of its present ruin? But that nothing may be wanting to its honor, I will add the number of its gates, and the multitude of its sacred relics; and that no person may complain of his being deprived of any knowledge by the obscurity of the narrative, the description shall run in an easy and familiar style.

The first is the Cornelian gate, which is now called the gate of St. Peter, and the Cornelian way. Near it is situated the church of St. Peter, in which his body lies, decked with gold and silver, and precious stones: and no one knows the number of the holy martyrs who rest in that church. On the same way is another church, in which lie the holy virgins Rufina and

Secunda. In a third church, are Marius and Martha, and Audi-
fax and Abacuc, their sons.

The second is the Flaminian gate, which is now called the
gate of St. Valentine, and the Flaminian way, and when it
arrives at the Milvian bridge, it takes the name of the Raven-
nanian way, because it leads to Ravenna; and there, at the
first stone without the gate, St. Valentine rests in his church.

The third is called the Porcinian gate, and the way the same;
but where it joins the Salarian, it loses its name, and there,
nearly in the spot which is called Cucumeris, lie the martyrs,
Festus, Johannes, Liberalis, Diogenes, Blastus, Lucina, and in
one sepulcher, the Two Hundred and Sixty, in another, the
Thirty.

The fourth is the Salarian gate and way; now called St.
Silvester's. Here, near the road, lie St. Hermes, and St. Vasella,
and Prothus, and Jacinctus, Maxilian, Herculan, Crispus; and,
in another place, hard by, rest the holy martyrs Pamphilus and
Quirinus, seventy steps beneath the surface. Next is the church
of St. Felicity, where she rests, and Silanus her son; and not far
distant, Boniface the martyr. In another church, there are
Crisantus, and Daria, and Saturninus, and Maurus, and Jason,
and their mother Hilaria, and others innumerable. And in an-
other church, St. Alexander, Vitalis, Martialis, sons of St.
Felicity; and seven holy virgins, Saturnina, Hilarina, Duranda,
Rogantina, Serotina, Paulina, Donata. Next the church of St.
Silvester, where he lies under a marble tomb; and the martyrs
Celestinus, Philippus, and Felix; and there too, the Three
Hundred and Sixty-five martyrs rest in one sepulcher; and near
them lie Paulus and Crescentianus, Prisca and Semetrius,
Praxides and Potentiana.

The fifth is called the Numentan gate. There lies St. Nico-
mede, priest and martyr; the way too is called by the same
name. Near the road are the church and body of St. Agnes;
in another church, St. Ermerenciana, and the martyrs, Alex-

ander, Felix, Papias; at the seventh stone on this road rests the holy pope Alexander, with Euentius and Theodolus.

The sixth is the Tiburtine gate and way, which is now called St. Lawrence's: near this way lies St. Lawrence in his church, and Habundius the martyr: and near this, in another church, rest these martyrs, Ciriaca, Romanus, Justinus, Crescentianus; and not far from hence the church of St. Hippolytus, where he himself rests, and his family, eighteen in number; there too repose, St. Trifonia, the wife of Decius, and his daughter Cirilla, and her nurse Concordia. And in another part of this way is the church of Apapit the martyr.

The seventh is called, at present, the Greater gate, formerly the Seracusan, and the way the Lavicanian, which leads to St. Helena. Near this are Peter, Marcellinus, Tyburtius, Geminus, Gorgonius, and the Forty Soldiers, and others without number; and a little farther the Four Coronati.

The eighth is the gate of St. John, which by the ancients was called Assenarica. The ninth gate is called Metrosa; and in front of both of these runs the Latin way. The tenth is called the Latin gate and way. Near this, in one church, lie the martyrs, Gordianus and Epimachus, Sulpicius, Servilianus, Quintinus, Quartus, Sophia, Triphenus. Near this too, in another spot, Tertullinus, and not far distant, the church of St. Eugenia, in which she lies, and her mother Claudia, and pope Stephen, with nineteen of his clergy, and Nemesius the deacon.

The eleventh is called the Appian gate and way. There lie St. Sebastian, and Quirinus, and originally the bodies of the apostles rested there. A little nearer Rome, are the martyrs, Januarius, Urbanus, Xenon, Quirinus, Agapetus, Felicissimus; and in another church, Tyburtius, Valerianus, Maximus. Not far distant is the church of the martyr Cecilia; and there are buried Stephanus, Sixtus, Zefferinus, Eusebius, Melchiades, Marcellus, Eutychianus, Dionysius, Antheros, Pontianus, pope Lucius, Optacius, Julianus, Calocerus, Parthenius, Tharsicius,

Politanus, martyrs: there too is the church and body of St. Cornelius: and in another church, St. Sotheris: and not far off, rest the martyrs, Hippolytus, Adrianus, Eusebius, Maria, Martha, Paulina, Valeria, Marcellus, and near, pope Marcus in his church. Between the Appian and Ostiensian way, is the Ardeatine way, where are St. Marcus, and Marcellianus. And there lies pope Damasus in his church; and near him St. Petronilla, and Nereus, and Achilleus, and many more.

The twelfth gate and way is called the Ostiensian, but, at present, St. Paul's, because he lies near it in his church. There too is the martyr Timotheus: and near, in the church of St. Tecla, are the martyrs Felix, Audactus, and Nemesius. At the Three Fountains is the head of the martyr St. Anastasius.

The thirteenth is called the Portuan gate and way; near which in a church are the martyrs, Felix, Alexander, Abdon and Sennes, Symeon, Anastasius, Polion, Vincentius, Milex, Candida, and Innocentia.

The fourteenth is the Aurelian gate and way, which now is called the gate of St. Pancras, because he lies near it in his church, and the other martyrs, Paulinus, Arthemius, St. Sapientia, with her three daughters, Faith, Hope, and Charity. In another church, Processus and Martinianus; and, in a third, two Felixes; in a fourth Calixtus, and Calepodius; in a fifth St. Basilides. At the twelfth milliary within the city, on Mount Celius, are the martyrs Johannes, and Paulus, in their dwelling, which was made a church after their martyrdom: and Crispin and Cirspinianus, and St. Benedicta. On the same mount, is the church of St. Stephen, the first martyr; and there are buried the martyrs Primus, and Felicianus; on Mount Aventine St. Boniface; and on Mount Nola, St. Tatiana rests.

Such are the Roman sanctuaries; such the sacred pledges upon earth: and yet in the midst of this heavenly treasure, as it were, a people drunk with senseless fury, even at the very time the crusaders arrived,[3] were disturbing everything with wild ambition, and, when unable to satisfy their lust of money, pouring out the blood of their fellow citizens over the very bodies of the saints. . . .

1 *Aeneid* I, 282.

2 On this poem and on other evidence in the twelfth century of "certain attitudes toward the monumental remains of antiquity which may be characterized broadly as humanistic," see James Bruce Ross, "A Study of Twelfth-Century Interest in the Antiquities of Rome," in *Medieval and Historiographical Essays in Honor of James Westfall Thompson*, eds. J. L. Cate and E. N. Anderson (Chicago, 1938), pp. 302-321.

3 In 1097, taking part in the First Crusade.

GIOVANNI VILLANI

On Villani and several other Florentines, see the Appendix to this
volume.

This selection, and the one in the Appendix, are from Villani's
Chronicle, trans. Rose E. Selfe, ed. Philip H. Wicksteed, 2nd. ed.
(London, 1906). Reprinted with the kind permission of Constable
& Co. Ltd.

THE JUBILEE OF 1300
(*Chronicle* VIII, 36)

IN THE year of Christ 1300, according to the birth of Christ, inasmuch as it was held by many that after every hundred years from the nativity of Christ, the Pope which was reigning at the time granted great indulgences, Pope Boniface VIII, which then occupied the apostolic chair, in reverence for the nativity of Christ, granted supreme and great indulgences after this manner; that within the whole course of this said year, to whatsoever Roman should visit continuously for thirty days the churches of the Blessed Apostles S. Peter and S. Paul, and to all other people which were not Romans which should do likewise for fifteen days, there should be granted full and entire remission of all their sins, both the guilt and the punishment thereof, they having made or to make confession of the same. And for consolation of the Christian pilgrims, every Friday and every solemn feast day, was shown in S. Peter's the Veronica, the true image of Christ, on the napkin. For the which thing, a great part of the Christians which were living at that time, women as well as men, made the said pilgrimage from distant and divers countries, both from far and near. And it was the most marvellous thing that was ever seen, for throughout the year, without break, there were in Rome, besides the inhabitants of the city, 200,000 pilgrims, not counting those who were coming and going on their journeys; and all were suitably supplied and satisfied with provisions, horses as well as persons, and all was well ordered, and without tumult or strife; and I can bear witness to this, for I was present and saw it. And from the offerings made by the pilgrims much treasure was added to the Church, and all the Romans were enriched by the trade.

And I, finding myself on that blessed pilgrimage in the holy city of Rome, beholding the great and ancient things therein, and reading the stories and the great doings of the Romans, written by Virgil, and by Sallust, and by Lucan, and Titus Livius, and Valerius, and Paulus Orosius, and other masters of history, which wrote alike of small things as of great, of the deeds and actions of the Romans, and also of foreign nations throughout the world, myself to preserve memorials and give examples to those which should come after took up their style and design, although as a disciple I was not worthy of such a work. But considering that our city of Florence, the daughter and creature of Rome, was rising, and had great things before her, whilst Rome was declining, it seemed to me fitting to collect in this volume and new chronicle all the deeds and beginnings of the city of Florence, in so far as it has been possible for me to find and gather them together, and to follow the doings of the Florentines in detail, and the other notable things of the universe in brief, as long as it shall be God's pleasure; in hope of which, rather than in my own poor learning, I undertook, by his grace, the said enterprise; and thus in the year 1300, having returned from Rome, I began to compile this book, in reverence to God and the blessed John, and in commendation of our city of Florence.

PETRARCH

A book might well be written on "Petrarch and the Idea of Rome," for both the ancient Republic and contemporary Rome, deserted by the popes, figure large throughout his career. As a young man he edited Livy, as an old man he defended Rome and Italy against Gallic slanders; he encouraged Cola di Rienzo's bold attempt to revive the Republic, and the rather less fervent endeavors of the Holy Roman Emperor, Charles IV.

There are recent biographies of Petrarch by E. H. Wilkins (Chicago, 1961) and Morris Bishop (Bloomington, 1963). On aspects of his interest in Rome: M. E. Cosenza, Francesco Petrarca and the Revolution of Cola di Rienzo (Chicago, 1913); and Aldo Bernardo, Petrarch, Scipio and the 'Africa': The Birth of Humanism's Dream (Baltimore, 1962). On his view of history, see Theodor E. Mommsen, "Petrarch's Conception of the 'Dark Ages,'" reprinted in Medieval and Renaissance Studies, ed. Eugene F. Rice, Jr. (Ithaca: reissued 1966), pp. 106-129; and Hans Baron, "The Evolution of Petrarch's Thought: Reflections on the State of Petrarch Studies," reprinted in From Petrarch to Leonardo Bruni (Chicago & London, 1968), pp. 7-50.

FIRST IMPRESSIONS OF ROME

WHAT may you expect from Rome, after my long letter from the mountains?[1] You thought I would write something fine when I should reach Rome. No doubt I have accumulated a lot of matter to write about later, but at present I am so overwhelmed and stunned by the abundant marvels that I shouldn't dare to begin. But this I shouldn't conceal: the reverse of your predictions has taken place. For I remember that you used to discourage me from making the journey, arguing that my ardor would cool on seeing a ruined city, falling short of its reputation and of my expectation based on my reading. I too, though afire with desire, was willing to defer my visit, fearing that the sight of actuality would bring low my high imaginations. Present reality is always hostile to greatness. But, remarkable to state, this presence has diminished nothing but has increased everything. Rome was greater than I thought, and so are its remains. Now I wonder not that the world was ruled by this city but that the rule came so late. Farewell.

[1] The present letter (*Ep. Fam.* II, 14) was written from Rome, 11 March 1337, to Petrarch's patron, Cardinal Giovanni Colonna. "Walks in Rome" is an excerpt from *Ep. Fam.* VI, 2 (of uncertain date), to Giovanni Colonna di San Vito, a Dominican monk who belonged to a minor branch of this noble family. (In supporting Cola di Rienzo, Petrarch was later to excoriate the Roman nobility as a major source of the city's woes.)

WALKS IN ROME

. . . YOU and I took our walks in that city, so great that in spite of its immense population it seems empty. We wandered not only in the city but around it, at every step happening on something to stir our thoughts and words. Here was the residence of Evander, here the house of Carmenta, here the cave of Cacus, here the nursing she-wolf and "ruminalis" fig tree of Romulus and Remus, which is better called "romularis"; here Remus died, here were the games of the circus, the rape of the Sabine women, the marsh of Capraea, the place where Romulus disappeared. Here Numa talked with Egeria; here was the Battle of the Triplets, Horatius and his brothers. Here the victorious organizer of the army, Tullus Hostilius, was struck down by lightning. Here lived Ancus Marcius, the builder-king; and here Priscus Tarquinius, the social legislator. Here fire descended on the head of Servius; here passed the abominable Tullia, sitting in her cart, and for her crime making the street infamous. But here is the Sacred Way, and the Esquiline, Viminal, Quirinal and Caelian hills; here is the Campus Martius, and here Tarquinius Superbus struck off the heads of the poppies. Here the unhappy Lucretia, escaping from her violation to death, fell upon her sword; here Brutus prepared vengeance for his offended honor. Here stood threatening Porsenna, and the Etruscan army, and Mucius, who punished his own right hand for its misdeed, and the tyrant's son at odds with liberty, and the consul who pursued the defeated enemy even to the lower world. Here is the Sublician Bridge, which a battling hero had broken down behind his back, and the Tiber, which bore fleeing Cloelia, and where Horatius swam across. Here was the house of Publicola, wrongly suspected; here Cincinnatus was plowing when he was summoned to be dictator; hence Serranus was carried off to be consul. This is the Janiculum, here is the Aventine, there the Sacred Hill, where three times the plebs revolted against the patricians. Here was the lewd tribunal of Appius, from whose lusts Virginia was saved by her father's sword, and the debaucheries of the decemvir came to a fitting end. Hence departed Coriolanus, mastered by filial piety, when perhaps he was on the edge of victory. Here is the cliff

defended by Manlius, whence he cast himself down. Here
Camillus repelled the Gauls, panting for gold; and here he
taught the despairing citizens that their abandoned country
could be recovered not by gold but by the sword. Here Curtius
threw himself down in full armor; here was found underground
the bust of a man, immovable, taken to be the presage of a
mighty, stable rule. Here the cheating Vestal, caught in her
own deceptions, was cut down. This is the Tarpeian Rock, and
the place where the worldwide census of the Roman people was
preserved. Here is the silver goose, and Janus, guardian of arms.
This is the temple of Jupiter Stator, that the shrine of Jupiter
Feretrius. This was Jove's earthly home, the goal of all triumphs.
From here Hannibal was thrown back, and Jugurtha (though
some say he was in fact killed in prison). Here Caesar triumphed, here he died. In this temple Augustus saw the kings of
earth prostrate and the world at his feet. This is the arch and
portico of Pompey, that the Cimbrian arch of Marius. There
stands the column of Trajan, to mark the grave of the only
Emperor (says Eusebius) who is buried within the city. There
is Trajan's bridge, which has taken the name of St. Peter; and
Hadrian's massive structure and tomb, now called Castel Sant'
Angelo. Observe that massive rock surmounted by bronze lions,
and sacred to the divine emperors. At its summit, they say, rest
the bones of Julius Caesar. Here are the Temples of the Earth-
Goddess, of Fortune, of Peace (which was overthrown at the
coming of the true King of Peace). There stands the work of
Agrippa, taken from the false gods to be dedicated to the mother
of the true God. Here it once snowed on the fifth of August;
here a rivulet of olive oil flowed into the Tiber; here, the story
goes, the Sibyl showed the infant Christ to the aged Augustus.
There is displayed insolent Nero's frantic luxury in building;
there on the via Flaminia stands the house of Augustus, where,
some say, the master lies buried. There is the column of An-
toninus, and close by the palace of Appius. And there the Sep-

tizonium of Severus Afrus, which you call the Palace of the Sun, but I find my name for it in the histories. On these stones the genius and art of Praxiteles and Phidias still contend for mastery.

And here Christ came to find his fleeing lieutenant; here Peter was crucified, Paul beheaded, Lawrence grilled; here the buried master made way for Stephen. Here John scorned the boiling oil; Agnes rose after death to forbid her kin to weep for her; here Silvester hid, Constantine was healed of his leprosy, Calixtus mounted his glorious bier.

But why continue? Can I fix Rome for you on this poor sheet of paper? And if I could, there is no need. You know all this, not because you are a Roman citizen, but because from boyhood you have been chiefly curious about such matters. For who today are more ignorant of the Roman story than are the citizens of Rome? I say it reluctantly: nowhere is Rome less known than in Rome. Therefore I bewail not ignorance alone —though what is worse than ignorance?—but the flight and exile of many virtues. For who can doubt that if Rome should commence to know itself it would rise again? However, I shall leave this complaint to another time.

Well then, when we were tired out by our long explorations of the city, we often used to rest at the Baths of Diocletian; and frequently we would climb up to the roof of that building, once so magnificent. No other place affords such a wide view, such brisk air, such silence and longed-for solitude. There we did not mention business, private matters, or public affairs—it was enough to have deplored them once. Sitting there, as when we had clambered on the walls of the crumbling city, we had the broken ruins under our eyes. We talked long of the city's history. We seemed to be divided; you seemed better informed in modern, I in ancient history. (Let us call "ancient" whatever preceded the celebration and veneration of Christ's name in Rome, "modern" everything from then to our own time.). . . .

ANTONIO MANETTI

In 1401 a competition was announced, the winner to design the northern doors of the Baptistry in Florence. Lorenzo Ghiberti (whose later doors, facing the Cathedral, Michelangelo is said to have called "the gates of Paradise") was chosen over Filippo Brunelleschi, who then retired to study the remains of Roman art.

Brunelleschi returned to become the outstanding architect of the early Renaissance. In 1418 he won the competition to construct the dome of the Cathedral (Santa Maria del Fiore), a stupendous architectural monument which occupied him from 1420 until 1434. Other famous designs were the Pazzi Chapel (in Santa Croce) and the Pitti Palace.

The first biography of Brunelleschi, written only a few years after his death in 1446, is ascribed to Antonio Manetti (1423-1491), a judge in the competition of 1491 for the façade of Santa Maria del Fiore. For an assessment of Brunelleschi within the context of Renaissance humanism, see Ernest H. Gombrich, "From the Revival of Letters to the Reform of the Arts," in Essays in the History of Art Presented to Rudolph Wittkower, ed. Douglas Fraser et al. (London, 1967), pp. 71-82. On the influence of the new ideas on Ghiberti: Gombrich, "The Renaissance Conception of Artistic Progress and its Consequences," in Norm and Form: Studies in the Art of the Renaissance (London, 1966), pp. 1-10.

From Literary Sources of Art History: An Anthology of Texts from Theophilus to Goethe, ed. Elizabeth Gilmore Holt (copyright 1947 by Princeton University Press), pp. 102-107. Reprinted by permission of Princeton University Press.

BRUNELLESCHI IN ROME
(*Vita di Filippo di Ser Brunellesco*)

. . . HAVING been rejected in this manner, it is almost as though Filippo said, "I did not know how to do well enough to have them put their confidence entirely in me; it would be a good thing to go and study where sculpture is really good." And so he went to Rome, for at that time there were plenty of good things that could be seen in public places. Some of the things are still there, though few. Many have since been stolen and carried away by various pontiffs and cardinals, Romans and men of other nations. While looking at the sculpture, as he had a good eye and an alert mind, he saw the way the ancients built and their proportions. As if he were enlightened concerning great things by God, he seemed to recognize quite clearly a certain order in their members and structural parts. This he noticed especially, for it looked very different from what was usual in those times. He proposed, while he was looking at the statues of the ancients, to devote no less attention to the order and method of building. And so he observed closely the supports and thrusts of the buildings, their forms, arches and inventions, according to the function they had to serve, as also their ornamental detail. In these he saw many wonders and beauties, for the buildings were made at various times and for the most part by good masters who became great because of their experience in building and because the rewards of the princes made it possible for them to study, and also because they were not uneducated men. Brunellesco proposed to rediscover the excellent and highly ingenious building methods of the ancients and their harmonious proportions and where such proportions could be used with ease and economy without detriment to the building.

Having perceived the great and difficult problems that had been solved in the Roman buildings, he was filled with no small desire to understand the methods they had adopted and with what tools [they had worked]. In the past he had made, for his pleasure, clocks and alarm clocks with various different types of springs put together from a variety of different contrivances. All or most of these springs and contrivances he had seen; which was a great help to him in imagining the various machines used for carrying, lifting, pulling, according to the occasions where he saw they had been necessary. He took notes or not, according to what he thought necessary. He saw some ruins, some still standing upright, and others which had been overthrown for various reasons. He studied the methods of centering the vaults and of other scaffolding, and also where one could do without them to save money and effort; and what method one would have to follow. Likewise, [he considered] cases where scaffolding cannot be used because the vault is too big and for various other reasons. He saw and considered many beautiful things which from those antique times, when good masters lived, until now had not been utilized by any others, as far as we know. Because of his genius, by experimenting and familiarizing himself with those methods, he secretly and with much effort, time and diligent thought, under the pretense of doing other than he did, achieved complete mastery of them, as he afterwards proved in our city and elsewhere, as will be shown in due time in the present narrative.

During this period in Rome he was almost continually with the sculptor Donatello. From the beginning they were in agreement concerning matters of sculpture more particularly, and to these they applied themselves continually. Donatello never opened his eyes to architecture. Filippo never told of his interest, either because he did not see any aptitude in Donatello or perhaps because he was himself not sure of his grasp, seeing his difficulties more clearly every moment. Nevertheless, together they made rough drawings of almost all the buildings in Rome, and in many places in the environs, with the measurements of the width, length and height, so far as they were able to ascertain them by judgment. In many places they had excavations done in order to see the joinings of the parts of the buildings and their nature, and whether those parts were square, polygonal or perfectly round, circular or oval, or of some other shape. And thus they were able to estimate the height from the bases and foundations to the cornices and the roofs of the buildings, they noted the measurements on strips of parchment like those used for squaring pages, with arithmetical numbers and characters which Filippo only understood. Since both were good goldsmiths they earned their livelihood by that trade; for at the workshops of the goldsmiths they were given more work than they could do. Filippo dressed many precious stones which he had been given to cut, set and polish. Neither was bothered by family cares and worries because neither had a wife nor children there or elsewhere. Neither was much concerned with how he ate, drank, lived or dressed himself, provided he could satisfy himself with these things to see and measure. Because they had to dig in many places in order to investigate structures or to find buildings where some indication was discernible that some buried edifice existed, it was necessary for them to hire porters and other laborers, and this at great expense, since no one else did the thing or understood why they did it. The reason why none understood why they did this was that at that time no one gave any thought to the ancient method of building, nor had for hundreds of years. In the time of the pagans some authors gave rules, as Battista Alberti did in our own time,[1] but these were little more than generalities. Constructive ideas which are peculiar to a master of their craft are necessarily the gift in large measure of nature or obtained through the master's own industry.

To return to the excavations of Filippo and Donato, they

were generally called the treasure-men, in the belief that they
were spending treasures and seeking them. It was said, those
treasure-men are searching today in this place and another time
in another place, etc. It is true that sometimes, although seldom, one finds in such excavations medals of silver and even of
gold, and also carved gems, calcedons, cameos, and similar
stones. This was the source of the belief that they were digging
for treasure. At such work Filippo spent many years. He found
in the decoration and adornment of the various buildings many
differences in the finish of the building blocks as well as in the
columns, bases, capitals, architraves, friezes, cornices and pediments, in the shapes and styles of temples and in the thickness
of the columns. From these observations, with his keen vision,
he began to distinguish the characteristics of each style, such as
Ionic, Doric, Tuscan, Corinthian and Attic, and he used those
styles at the times and places he thought best, as one may still
see in his buildings.

And since not everyone is informed on the origins of these
building methods known as "in the antique style," I shall go
back a little by way of digression, if you have no objection, to
make the matter clearer to you as I promised, so that you may
learn of this before I come to Filippo's architectural works that
were started after his return from Rome as well as those that he
built after that, for which he merited much praise. . . .

The art of building in the said manner arose, like all other
methods, from the quite lowly and rude structures of the earliest
peoples, necessarily simple, to avoid cold and heat and wind and
rain, such as cabins and houses of rude poles covered with
boughs and straw as nature provided, and made of earth, some
of plain stones, or later, stones and earth for want of mortar. And
from this they advanced to pitch that they found, which is
naturally produced in some countries; and since it was not
everywhere, men began to develop inventiveness, gaining experience with the passing of time. Thus by chance, through

burning, lime mortar was discovered, and since economy did not worsen it, the admixture of sand; and where there were no stones, brick was discovered, for everywhere in the world there is earth. And from using rough stones just as they were dug they advanced to shaping them somewhat so as to join those that did not fit of themselves; and from this to dressed stone, for in doing one thing another is suggested. These stones thus dressed [that is, stone dressed on its exposed face] were a slight beginning of luxury; and as wealth and principalities arose they took up the luxurious, for the sake of glory and ostentation and to excite admiration and produce ease and comfort, and from this to making what would enclose and defend treasures and kingdoms. One can see that these things came first where there were first principalities and wealth; and so we find that the Pyramids and the Labyrinth of Egypt are the oldest. It is irrelevant here whether the Tartars are earlier than the Egyptians in respect to fire and water, for the Tartars do not use walled dwellings, and the peoples in their countries have no fixed stopping place. And from here there was a shift into Assyria and various kingdoms of Asia and, after many transformations, from there into Europe and especially into various republics and principalities in Greece. Here building prospered greatly because of the great talents and judgment of the worthy men that were there, for it may be called the source of philosophy and philosophers, who in the fulness of time would reject or accept, knowing what was best to be done, and what to be left. And since Greece prospered at various places and times, according to the nature of the people who arose, various manners of building were approved, contributing for periods to ornaments, fortification, and the durability of architecture; and because in each place men of authority favored their own craftsmen and their talents, and because the one did not wish to show that he derived a system from the other, or was inferior to him, many various and differing manners took root there, as may be seen in the classification of columns cited above and in their literature. From secular public buildings they proceeded to churches and temples and various tributes to the gods.

In Asia, before Greek minds and talents appeared, for a long time building was rude and undefined, rich and sumptuous rather than ordered, aside from the things of the Hebrews, people chosen of God, who through the prophets and in other like ways were inspired with the general and particular forms and conditions of the will of God. But the first plans and orders to become civilized were, it may be said, at Ephesus in Asia, in the wonderful and very rich Temple of Diana, whose architect was Ctesiphon. And here and by him, it is said, bases were first placed under columns and capitals over them. But the way in which the advance was made from the disorder of that early period to more civil things seems to have been thus: that just as pitch, mortar and the dressing of stone had been discovered, so were walls, pilasters and columns achieved, in which, however, great disorderliness could not but appear, since the orders were not yet in use. In this disorderliness, as it happened, one element was more censurable than another, and when the most censurable had been removed and avoided, they came to the second, third, fourth, and so on, whence arose the plumb line, the plumet, the square, and various instruments.

And in removing the irregularities, there appeared in the less displeasing remainder a something that gave pleasure; and in this pleasure, furthermore, one thing was more pleasing than another. Thus was begun to be discovered a certain amount of system in things; that is, a system appropriate to these things. This system meant a complex of things from which everything had been removed that displeased. And one must assume that architraves, friezes, cornices, pediments, moulding and piers were wooden and rude at first, without any ornament, but simple, as nature provided, since, as was said, these thing first grew from necessity. Thus the columns were without bases or cap-

itals, for they were originally timber for an upright or for a trans-
verse beam, as was needed. And in said temple of Ephesian
Diana that most unusual architect first of all found a way of
arranging matters and thus were formulated the first rules for
entirely avoiding the unsuitable and arriving at praiseworthy
orders. And many things, as they say, which prospered wonderfully in Greece, in the shifting of power from Greece to Rome,
shifted to the Romans and to that illustrious city that was the
mistress of the world. And since architects go and are drawn to
places where there is money and kingdoms and a readiness to
spend, with the power of Greece, the architects also shifted, for
obtaining no return in Greece they sought it where power and
wealth were. Hence in Rome the masters prospered far more
wonderfully than in Greece, as wealth and experience grew so
wonderfully. And there [the art] reached such a condition and
fame and such wonder that the mere ruins and the small rem-
nants are most astounding.

And as it happened in other places, so here: when the Empire
declined, architecture and architects declined, and when the
barbarian tribes of the Vandals, Goths, Lombards and Huns,
and others came, they brought their architects with them, and
for centuries they built in their own ways in the countries where
they were lords. And because the tribes from far away had no
talent fitted for these things, they drew on their nearest neighbors, by whom they were most followed after, and especially on
Germany. Here there have always been many craftsmen and
active men, and they went along with the victors just across the
borders. For they [the Germans] bounded almost all these tribes
on one side and another, and wherever these [the Germans]
ruled they built in their own way. All private, secular and sacred
buildings were made in their style and they filled all Italy with
them, and various countries beyond the mountains. But when
the last, which were Lombards, were driven away by Charlemagne, and Italy was purged of them, and when Charlemagne

came to an agreement with the popes of Rome and such of the Roman republics as existed, he also drew with him the architects of the Roman and papal regions, men not very expert, for want of practice. But still they built in that way because they had been born among those things and had seen nothing else; and since Charlemagne had our city re-established and restored by architects whom he brought with him, one may see some little reflection of the splendor of those ancient buildings of Rome, as in S. Piero Scheraggio and Santi Apostoli, which are and were his buildings. And because the dynasty of Charlemagne lasted through few generations and the Empire came into German hands, the manner which had returned by means of Charlemagne largely disappeared, and the German ways of building revived again and lasted until our century,—to the time of Filippo. . . .

---

1 The Architecture of Leon Battista Alberti, trans. Giac. Leoni (London, 1726). His Della Pittura is dedicated to Brunelleschi, whom—along with Donatello, Ghiberti, Luca della Robbia and Masaccio—he ranks with the best ancient artists. On Alberti's own architectural practice, see Rudolph Wittkower, "Alberti's Approach to Antiquity in Architecture," Journal of the Warburg and Courtauld Institutes IV (1941), 1-18.

JACOB BURCKHARDT

Though often severely criticized, Burckhardt's essay on the Renaissance (first published in 1860) remains an influential and essential part of the literature. A fine recent assessment of his work is provided by Benjamin Nelson and Charles Trinkaus in the Harper Torchbook reprint (1958). See also Jacob Burckhardt and the Renaissance 100 Years After, published by the Museum of Art at the University of Kansas (April, 1960). On interpretations of the Renaissance the standard work is Wallace K. Ferguson, The Renaissance in Historical Thought (Cambridge, Mass., 1948), much of which is naturally devoted to Burckhardt and the tradition he established.

From The Civilization of the Renaissance in Italy, trans. S. G. C. Middlemore (London: Allen & Unwin; New York: Macmillan). First edition, 1878; second edition, 1890; ninth impression, 1928. The notes of Burckhardt and his various editors have been omitted.

ROME, THE CITY OF RUINS

(The Civilization of the Renaissance in Italy:
Part III: The Revival of Antiquity, Ch. ii)

ROME itself, the city of ruins, now became the object of a
wholly different sort of piety from that of the time when the
Mirabilia Romae[1] and the collection of William of Malmesbury were composed. The imagination of the devout pilgrim, or
of the seeker after marvels and treasures, are supplanted in contemporary records by the interests of the patriot and the historian. In this sense we must understand Dante's words, that
the stones of the walls of Rome deserve reverence, and that the
ground on which the city is built is more worthy than men say.
The jubilees, incessant as they were, have scarcely left a single
devout record in literature properly so called. The best thing
that Giovanni Villani brought back from the jubilee of the year
1300 was the resolution to write his history which had been
awakened in him by the sight of the ruins of Rome. Petrarch
gives evidence of a taste divided between classical and Christian
antiquity. He tells us how often with Giovanni Colonna he
ascended the mighty vaults of the Baths of Diocletian, and there
in the transparent air, amid the wide silence, with the broad
panorama stretching far around them, they spoke, not of business or political affairs, but of the history which the ruins beneath their feet suggested, Petrarch appearing in their dialogues
as the partisan of classical, Giovanni of Christian antiquity;
then they would discourse of philosophy and of the inventors of
the arts. How often since that time, down to the days of Gibbon
and Niebuhr, have the same ruins stirred men's minds to the
same reflections!

This double current of feeling is also recognizable in the *Dittamondo* of Fazio degli Uberti, composed about the year 1360—a description of visionary travels, in which the author is accompanied by the old geographer Solinus, as Dante was by Virgil. They visit Bari in memory of St. Nicholas, and Monte Gargano of the archangel Michael, and in Rome the legends of Araceli and of Santa Maria in Trastevere are mentioned. Still, the pagan splendor of ancient Rome unmistakably exercises a greater charm upon them. A venerable matron in torn garments —Rome herself is meant—tells them of the glorious past, and gives them a minute description of the old triumphs; she then leads the strangers through the city, and points out to them the seven hills and many of the chief ruins—"che comprender potrai, quanto fui bella."

Unfortunately this Rome of the schismatic and Avignonese popes was no longer, in respect of classical remains, what it had been some generations earlier. The destruction of 140 fortified houses of the Roman nobles by the senator Brancaleone in 1257 must have wholly altered the character of the most important buildings then standing; for the nobles had no doubt ensconced themselves in the loftiest and best-preserved of the ruins. Nevertheless, far more was left than we now find, and probably many of the remains had still their marble incrustation, their pillared entrances, and their other ornaments, where we now see nothing but the skeleton of brickwork. In this state of things, the first beginning of a topographical study of the old city was made.

In Poggio's walks through Rome the study of the remains themselves is for the first time more intimately combined with that of the ancient authors and inscriptions—the latter he sought out from among all the vegetation in which they were imbedded—the writer's imagination is severely restrained, and the memories of Christian Rome carefully excluded.[2] The only pity is that Poggio's work was not fuller and was not illustrated

with sketches. Far more was left in his time than was found by
Raphael eighty years later. He saw the tomb of Caecilia Metella
and the columns in front of one of the temples on the slope of
the Capitol first in full preservation, and then afterwards half
destroyed, owing to that unfortunate quality which marble
possesses of being easily burnt into lime. A vast colonnade near
the Minerva fell piecemeal a victim to the same fate. A witness
in the year 1443 tells us that this manufacture of lime still went
on; "which is a shame, for the new buildings are pitiful, and the
beauty of Rome is in its ruins." The inhabitants of that day, in
their peasants' cloaks and boots, looked to foreigners like cow-
herds; and in fact the cattle were pastured in the city up to the
Banchi. The only opportunities for social gatherings were the
services at church, on which occasion it was possible to get a
sight of the beautiful women.

In the last years of Eugenius IV (d. 1447) Blondus of Forli
wrote his *Roma Instaurata*, making use of Frontinus and of the
old *Libri Regionali*, as well as, it seems, of Anastasius. His object
is not only the description of what existed, but still more the
recovery of what was lost. In accordance with the dedication to
the Pope, he consoles himself for the general ruin by the
thought of the precious relics of the saints in which Rome was
so rich.

With Nicholas V (1447-1455) that new monumental spirit
which was distinctive of the age of the Renaissance appeared on
the papal throne. The new passion for embellishing the city
brought with it on the one hand a fresh danger for the ruins, on
the other a respect for them, as forming one of Rome's claims to
distinction. Pius II was wholly possessed by antiquarian enthusiasm, and if he speaks little of the antiquities of Rome, he
closely studied those of all other parts of Italy, and was the first
to know and describe accurately the remains which abounded
in the districts for miles around the capital. It is true that, both
as priest and cosmographer, he is interested alike in classical

and Christian monuments and in the marvels of nature. Or was
he doing violence to himself when he wrote that Nola was more
highly honored by the memory of St. Paulinus than by all its
classical reminiscences and by the heroic struggle of Marcellus?
Not, indeed, that his faith in relics was assumed; but his mind
was evidently rather disposed to an inquiring interest in nature
and antiquity, to a zeal for monumental works, to a keen and
delicate observation of human life. In the last years of his
Papacy, afflicted with the gout and yet in the most cheerful
mood, he was borne in his litter over hill and dale to Tusculum,
Alba, Tibur, Ostia, Falerii, and Otriculum, and whatever he saw
he noted down. He followed the line of the Roman roads and
aqueducts, and tried to fix the boundaries of the old tribes who
dwelt round the city. On an excursion to Tivoli with the great
Federigo of Urbino the time was happily spent in talk on the
military system of the ancients, and particularly on the Trojan
war. Even on his journey to the Congress of Mantua (1459) he
searched, though unsuccessfully, for the labyrinth of Clusium
mentioned by Pliny, and visited the so-called villa of Virgil on
the Mincio. That such a Pope should demand a classical Latin
style from his abbreviators, is no more than might be expected.
It was he who, in the war with Naples, granted an amnesty to
the men of Arpinum, as countrymen of Cicero and Marius,
after whom many were named. It was to him alone, as both
judge and patron, that Blondus could dedicate his Roma Tri-
umphans, the first great attempt at a complete exposition of
Roman antiquity.

Nor was enthusiasm for the classical past of Italy confined at
this period to the capital. Boccaccio had already called the vast
ruins of Baiae "old walls, yet new for modern spirits"; and since
this time they were held to be the most interesting sight near
Naples. Collections of antiquities of all sorts now became common. Ciriaco of Ancona (d. 1457), who explained (1433) the
Roman monuments to the Emperor Sigismund, travelled, not

only through Italy, but through other countries of the old
world, Hellas, and the islands of the Archipelago, and even parts
of Asia and Africa, and brought back with him countless inscriptions and sketches. When asked why he took all this
trouble, he replied, "To wake the dead." The histories of the
various cities of Italy had from the earliest times laid claim to
some true or imagined connection with Rome, had alleged some
settlement or colonization which started from the capital; and
the obliging manufacturers of pedigrees seem constantly to have
derived various families from the oldest and most famous blood
of Rome. So highly was the distinction valued, that men clung
to it even in the light of the dawning criticism of the fifteenth
century. When Pius II was at Viterbo, he said frankly to the
Roman deputies who begged him to return, "Rome is as much
at home in Siena, for my House, Piccolomini, came in early
times from the capital to Siena, as is proved by the constant use
of the names Aeneas and Sylvius in my family." He would
probably have had no objection to be held a descendant of the
Julii. Paul II, a Barbo of Venice, found his vanity flattered by
deducing his House, notwithstanding an adverse pedigree, according to which it came from Germany, from the Roman
Ahenobarbus, who led a colony to Parma, and whose successors
were driven by party conflict to migrate to Venice. That the
Massimi claimed descent from Q. Fabius Maximus, and the
Cornaro from the Cornelii, cannot surprise us. On the other
hand, it is a strikingly exceptional fact for the sixteenth century
that the novellist Bandello tried to connect his blood with a
noble family of Ostrogoths.

To return to Rome. The inhabitants, "who called themselves
Romans," accepted greedily the homage which was offered
them by the rest of Italy. Under Paul II, Sixtus IV, and Alexander VI, magnificent processions formed part of the Carnival,
representing the scene most attractive to the imagination of the
time—the triumph of the Roman Imperator. The sentiment

of the people expressed itself naturally in this shape and others like it. In this mood of public feeling, a report arose, that on April 15, 1485, the corpse of a young Roman lady of the classical period—wonderfully beautiful and in perfect preservation—had been discovered. Some Lombard masons digging out an ancient tomb on an estate of the convent of Santa Maria Novella, on the Appian Way beyond the tomb of Caecilia Metella, were said to have found a marble sarcophagus with the inscription, "Julia, daughter of Claudius." On this basis the following story was built. The Lombards disappeared with the jewels and treasure which were found with the corpse in the sarcophagus. The body had been coated with an antiseptic essence, and was as fresh and flexible as that of a girl of fifteen the hour after death. It was said that she still kept the colors of life, with eyes and mouth half open. She was taken to the palace of the "Conservatori" on the Capitol; and then a pilgrimage to see her began. Among the crowd were many who came to paint her; "for she was more beautiful than can be said or written, and, were it said or written, it would not be believed by those who had not seen her." By the order of Innocent VIII she was secretly buried one night outside the Pincian Gate; the empty sarcophagus remained in the court of the "Conservatori." Probably a colored mask of wax or some other material was modelled in the classical style on the face of the corpse, with which the gilded hair of which we read would harmonize admirably. The touching point in the story is not the fact itself, but the firm belief that an ancient body, which was now thought to be at last really before men's eyes, must of necessity be far more beautiful than anything of modern date.

Meanwhile the material knowledge of old Rome was increased by excavations. Under Alexander VI the so-called "Grotesques," that is, the mural decorations of the ancients, were discovered, and the Apollo of the Belvedere was found at Porto d'Anzo. Under Julius II followed the memorable discoveries of the Laöcoon, of the Venus of the Vatican, of the Torso, of the Cleopatra. The palaces of the nobles and the cardinals began to be filled with ancient statues and fragments. Raphael undertook for Leo X that ideal restoration of the whole ancient city which his celebrated letter (1518 or 1519) speaks of.[3] After a bitter complaint over the devastations which had not even then ceased, he beseeches the Pope to protect the few relics which were left to testify to the power and greatness of that divine soul of antiquity whose memory was inspiration to all who were capable of higher things. He then goes on with penetrating judgment to lay the foundations of a comparative history of art, and concludes by giving the definition of an architectural survey which has been accepted since his time; he requires the ground plan, section, and elevation separately of every building that remained. How archaeology devoted itself after his day to the study of the venerated city and grew into a special science, and the Vitruvian Academy at all events proposed to itself great aims, cannot here be related. Let us rather pause at the days of Leo X, under whom the enjoyment of antiquity combined with all other pleasures to give to Roman life a unique stamp and consecration. The Vatican resounded with song and music, and their echoes were heard through the city as a call to joy and gladness, though Leo did not succeed thereby in banishing care and pain from his own life, and his deliberate calculation to prolong his days by cheerfulness was frustrated by an early death. The Rome of Leo, as described by Paolo Giovio, forms a picture too splendid to turn away from, unmistakable as are also its darker aspects—the slavery of those who were struggling to rise; the secret misery of the prelates, who, notwithstanding heavy debts, were forced to live in a style befitting their rank; the system of literary patronage, which drove men to be parasites or adventurers; and, lastly, the scandalous maladministration of the finances of the state. Yet the same Ariosto who knew and ridiculed all this so well, gives in the sixth satire a longing picture of his expected intercourse with the accomplished poets who would conduct him through the city of ruins, of the learned counsel which he would there find for his own literary efforts, and of the treasures of the Vatican library. These, he says, and not the long-abandoned hope of Medicean protection, were the real baits which attracted him, when he was asked to go as Ferrarese ambassador to Rome.

But the ruins within and outside Rome awakened not only archaeological zeal and patriotic enthusiasm, but an elegiac or sentimental melancholy. In Petrarch and Boccaccio we find touches of this feeling. Poggio often visited the temple of Venus and Rome, in the belief that it was that of Castor and Pollux, where the senate used so often to meet, and would lose himself in memories of the great orators Crassus, Hortensius, Cicero. The language of Pius II, especially in describing Tivoli, has a thoroughly sentimental ring, and soon afterwards (1467) appeared the first pictures of ruins, with a commentary by Polifilo. Ruins of mighty arches and colonnades, half hid in plane-trees, laurels, cypresses, and brushwood, figure in his pages. In the sacred legends it became the custom, we can hardly say how, to lay the scene of the birth of Christ in the ruins of a magnificent palace. That artificial ruins became afterwards a necessity of landscape gardening, is only a practical consequence of this feeling.

---

1 The *Mirabilia* (ca. 1140), along with later accretions, may be read in an English translation by Francis Morgan Nichols (London & Rome, 1889).

2 For Poggio on the ruins of Rome, see *The Portable Renaissance Reader*, eds. J. B. Ross and M. M. McLaughlin (New York, 1953; often reprinted), pp. 379-384.

3 There is a translation of this letter (which was probably written with Castiglione's collaboration) in *A Documentary History of Art, Volume I: The Middle Ages & the Renaissance*, ed. Elizabeth G. Holt (Doubleday Anchor Book), pp. 289-296.

APPENDIX: ROME AND FLORENCE

Another, drawing tresses from her distaff,
Told o'er among her family the tales
Of Trojans and of Fesole and Rome.
As great a marvel then would have been held
A Lapo Salterello, a Cianghella,
As Cincinnatus or Cornelia now.

Dante, *Paradiso* XV, 124-129 (trans. Longfellow)

GIOVANNI VILLANI

Villani's major source was a Chronica de origine civitatis composed around 1200. That first history of early Florence has the city twice founded by Romans: first as revenge against the Fiesolans, later as a reply to the challenge of Totila, who allegedly destroyed Florence some five centuries after its original founding.

Though the whole story of Totila is an invention, Florence does seem to have been founded by Romans during the first century B.C. Medieval Florence, like several other cities, traced its foundation to Julius Caesar; but later the humanist chancellor of Florence, Coluccio Salutati, proposed a more decidedly republican origin, and Rubinstein's interpretation of the sources points in the same direction. On Villani and his forerunners: Nicolai Rubinstein, "The Beginnings of Political Thought in Florence," Journal of the Warburg and Courtauld Institutes V (1942), 198-227.

THE BUILDING OF FLORENCE

(Chronicle I, 38)

AFTER the city of Fiesole was destroyed, Caesar with his armies descended to the plain on the banks of the river Arno, where Florinus and his followers had been slain by the Fiesolans, and in this place began to build a city, in order that Fiesole should never be rebuilt; and he dismissed the Latin horsemen whom he had with him, enriched with the spoils of Fiesole; and these Latins were called Tudertines. Caesar, then, having fixed the boundaries of the city, and included two places called Camarti and Villa Arnina [of the Arno], purposed to call it Caesaraea from his own name. But when the Roman senate heard this, they would not suffer Caesar to call it after his name, but they made a decree and order that the other chief noble Romans who had taken part in the seige of Fiesole should go and build the new city together with Caesar, and afterwards populate it; and that whichever of the builders first completed his share of the work should call it after his own name, or howso else it pleased him.

Then Macrinus, Albinus, Gnaeus Pompey, and Marcius, furnished with materials and workmen, came from Rome to the city which Caesar was building, and agreed with Caesar to divide the work after this manner: that Albinus undertook to pave all the city, which was a noble work and gave beauty and charm to the city, and to this day fragments of the work are found, in digging, especially in the sesto of Santo Piero Scheraggio, and in Porta San Piero, and in Porta del Duomo, where it shows that the ancient city was. Macrinus caused the water to be brought in conduits and aqueducts, bringing it from a distance of seven miles from the city, to the end the city might have abundance of good water to drink and to cleanse the city; and this conduit was carried from the river called Marina at the foot of Montemorello, gathering to itself all the springs above Sesto and Quinto and Colonnata. And in Florence the said springs came to a head at a great palace which was called *caput aquae*, but afterwards in our speech it was called Capaccia, and the remains can be seen in the Terma until this day. And note that the ancients, for health's sake, used to drink spring waters brought in by conduits, forasmuch as they were purer and more wholesome than water from wells; seeing that few, indeed very few, drank wine, but the most part water from conduits, but not from wells; and as yet there were very few wines. Gnaeus Pompey caused the walls of the city to be built of burnt bricks, and upon the walls of the city he built many round towers, and the space between one tower and the other was twenty cubits, and it was so that the towers were of great beauty and strength. Concerning the size and circuit of the city we can find no chronicle which makes mention thereof; save that when Totila, the scourge of God, destroyed it, history records that it was very great. Marcius, the other Roman lord, caused the Capitol to be built after the fashion of Rome, that is to say the palace, or master fortress of the city, and this was of marvellous beauty; into which the water of the river Arno came by a hollowed and vaulted passage, and returned into the Arno underground; and the city, at every festival, was cleansed by the outpouring of this duct. This Capitol stood where today is the piazza which is called the Mercato Vecchio, over against the church which is called S. Maria, in Campidoglio. This seems to be the best supported opinion; but some say that it was where the place is now called the Guardingo [citadel]; beside the Piazza di Popolo (so called from the Priors' Palace), which was another fortress. Guardingo was the name afterwards given to the remains of the walls and arches after the destruction by Totila, where the bad quarter was. And the said lords each strove to be in advance of the work of the others. And at one same time the whole was completed, so that to none of them was the favor granted of naming the city according to his desire, but by many it was at first called "Little Rome." Others called it Floria, because Florinus, who was the first builder in that spot, had there died, he being the fiore [flower] of warlike deeds and of chivalry, and because in the country and fields around where the city was built there always grew flowers and lilies. Afterwards the greater part of the inhabitants consented to call it Floria, as being built among flowers, that is, amongst many delights. And of a surety it was, inasmuch as it was peopled by the best of Rome, and the most capable, sent by the senate in due proportion from each division of Rome, chosen by lot from the inhabitants; and they admitted among their number those Fiesolans which desired there to dwell and abide. But afterwards it was, through long use of the vulgar tongue, called Fiorenza, that is "flowery sword." And we find that it was built in the year 682, after the building of Rome and seventy years before the birth of our Lord Jesus Christ. And note that it is not to be wondered at that the Florentines are always at war and strife among themselves, being born and descended from two peoples so contrary and hostile and different in habits as were the noble Romans in their virtue and the rude Fiesolans fierce in war.[1]

---

[1] On the change from Villani's view to Bruni's, see now Ronald Witt, "Coluccio Salutati and the Origins of Florence," Il Pensiero Politico II (1969), 161-172.

DANTE

In 1308 Henry of Luxembourg was elected Emperor (becoming
Henry VII); and in 1310, with the approval of the Pope, he set out
to pacify Italy. To Dante, the ancient Romans had been a chosen
people, appointed by God to make the world ready for Christ's advent; and since he viewed the contemporary empire as the direct heir
of the ancient, he ardently supported Henry, Italy's "bridegroom"
(Letter V), who would restore peace and justice to a troubled world.
(The De Monarchia was written during Henry's brief reign, which
ended with his death in 1313.)

When Florence, the "most beautiful daughter of Rome" (Con-
vivio I, iii) refused homage to Henry, Dante addressed to the Florentines a violent letter, the only result of which seems to have been
their banishing him from the city forever (1311). The next year, after
being crowned in Rome, Henry returned to Tuscany and attacked
Florence, unsuccessfully.

Henry was the last emperor who seriously tried to make Italy an
integral part of the Holy Roman Empire; and as Bowsky has concluded: "The expedition of Henry VII definitively discredited the
medieval imperial solution to Italy's problems. It marked the end of
a major chapter in Italian political history—as the victory of the city-
state, western kingdoms, and Avignon Papacy hastened the approaching Renaissance" (p. 211).

See William M. Bowsky, Henry VII in Italy: The Conflict of Em-
pire and City-State, 1310-1313 (Lincoln, 1960); Charles Till Davis,
Dante and the Idea of Rome (Oxford, 1957); and A. P. d'Entrèves,
Dante as a Political Thinker (Oxford, 1952).

From A Translation of Dante's Eleven Letters, by Charles Sterrett
Latham (Cambridge, 1892).

FLORENCE VERSUS ROME
(Letter VI, 1-3, 6: "Dante Alighieri, a Florentine and undeservedly an exile, to those most infamous Florentines within the city")

THE compassionate providence of the Eternal King, who, while in His goodness He perpetuates His celestial kingdom, does not in disdain desert our earthly one, decreed that human affairs should be governed by the Holy Empire of the Romans, in order that mankind might repose in the calm of so great a protection, and that it might everywhere be ruled agreeably to law, according to the demands of nature. Although this truth is confirmed by divine word, although antiquity supported by the prop of reason alone affirms this, nevertheless it is in no slight degree commended, in that, when the throne of Augustus is vacant, all the world swerves from the right way. For the helmsman and the rowers in the bark of Peter sleep, and Italy, wretched, alone, abandoned to private rule, and destitute of all public government, is struck by a force of wind and wave so great that words cannot describe it; yea, even the unfortunate Italians can scarcely measure it with their tears. Therefore let the faces of all who with foolhardy presumption haughtily oppose this most manifest will of God—even though the sword of Him who saith "Vengeance is mine"[1] has not yet fallen from heaven—be overspread with pallor, for already the sentence of the severe Judge hangs over them.

But you who transgress laws, human and divine, you whom the awful insatiability of avarice has led to be ready for any crime, does not the terror of the second death harass you, in that ye, first and alone, dreading the yoke of liberty, have raged against the glory of the Roman Prince, the monarch of the earth and the ambassador of God; and using the right of prescription, repudiating the duty of vassalage, have chosen rather to rise up in the madness of rebellion! Are ye ignorant, ye fools and licentious, that public justice will end with the end of time alone, and can be subject to the computation of no prescription? Surely the articles of the laws most loudly declare,

and human reason on examination pronounces, that the public rule
of affairs, though neglected ever so long, can never pass away, or,
however weakened, be conquered. For what happens to the advantage of all cannot perish or even be weakened without detriment to
all. Neither God nor nature wills this; and the general opinion of
mankind would hold it altogether in abhorrence. Why, then, such a
foolish supposition being disposed of, do ye, deserting the legitimate
government, seek like new Babylonians to found new kingdoms, in
order that the Florentines may be one polity and the Roman
another? Why may it not please you to envy the apostolic monarchy
likewise? that if Delia is to have a twin in heaven, the Delian One
may also.² If, however, thinking over your evil emprise does not
cause you alarm, let this, at least, terrify your hardened hearts: that
in punishment for your crime not only wisdom, but the beginning
of wisdom, has been taken away from you. For no condition of an
offender is more terrible than that of him who shamelessly and without fear of God does whatever he pleases; and, in truth, the evil
man is often smitten with this punishment, that he who has been
forgetful of God while he lived, in dying is forgetful of himself.

But if your insolent arrogance has rendered you, like the summits
of Gilboa, so entirely incapable of receiving the heavenly dew that
no fear has restrained you from resisting the decrees of the eternal
senate,—nor even yet are ye afraid for that ye did not fear,—can ye
free yourselves from that baneful terror, which is, in truth, human
and worldly, while the inevitable shipwreck of your most haughty
race, and your rapine, worthy of many tears, is hastening on? Do ye
because encircled by a ridiculous palisade trust to any defences whatever? O ye concordant for evil! O ye blinded by marvellous avarice!
In what will it profit you to have surrounded yourselves with a
wall,³ to have fortified yourselves with ramparts and battlements,
when the eagle, terrible in a field of gold, swoops down on you,—the
eagle who, now smiling over the Pyrenees, now over the Caucasus,
now over Atlas, the more strengthened by the opposition of the host
of heaven, of old looked down upon the vast seas as no hindrance to
his flight? How will ye stand amazed, O most wretched among men,
in the presence of the conqueror of raving Hesperia! In truth, the
hope which ye cherish in vain and without reason will receive no

advantage from your resistance; but by this obstacle will the advent
of the just king be inflamed the more, and compassion, always an
attendant on his army, will fly away in anger; and where ye think to
defend the role of a false liberty, there will ye fall into the bonds of
a true slavery. For it must be believed that it is sometimes brought
to pass by the wonderful judgment of God, that where the ungodly
thinks to shun a merited punishment, there is he precipitated into
it the more deeply; and he who has resisted the divine will know-
ingly and willingly, serves it unknowingly and unwillingly. . . .

O most wretched descendants of the Fiesolans! O Punic barbarity
once more renewed! Do these foretastes inspire you with a little fear?
Indeed, I believe ye tremble while awake, although ye feign hope in
your mien and in your lying speech, and in your dreams ye awake
many a time, either in dread of the presages ye have had or to revolve
the counsels of the day. But if while trembling with good reason, ye
repent without sorrow your having acted with madness, in order that
the streams of fear and grief may unite in the bitterness of repentance, these facts now remain to be impressed on your minds: that
this standard-bearer of the Roman Empire, the divine and triumphant Henry, thirsting not for his private advantage, but for the
public good of the world, undertook each arduous enterprise for
us, partaking our hardships of his own free will, so that to him after
Christ, the prophet Isaiah pointed the finger of prophesy, when by
the revelation of the Holy Ghost he foretold: "Surely he hath borne
our griefs, and carried our sorrows."[4] Therefore, if ye do not wish
to dissemble, ye will see that the time is now at hand most bitterly
to repent your foolhardy presumption. But a late repentance will
not be productive of forgiveness from henceforth; nay, rather the
commencement of a seasonable punishment. For it is true that the
sinner is smitten that he may be converted without backsliding.

Written on the thirty-first of March, on the confines of Tuscany,
near the springs of the Arno, in the first year of the most auspicious
passage of the Emperor Henry into Italy.

---

1 Deuteronomy xxxii, 35.
2 On the moon:sun relationship of Empire and Papacy, cf. *De Monarchia* III,

iv & xvi. Later, at *Purgatorio* XVI, 107, Marco Lombardo calls them Rome's
"two suns."
3 Villani (*Chronicle* IX, 10) says the walls were Florence's salvation.
4 Isaiah liii, 4.

BOCCACCIO

*It says much about the contemporary outlook that Boccaccio not
only felt compelled to trace Dante's lineage back to the Romans,
but even dated his birth with reference to the Empire and to the
Papacy. Bruni, by contrast, had Dante born more in the context of
the city-state, "shortly after the return to Florence of the Guelphs,
who had been in exile because of the defeat at Montaperti" (p. 82);
and he considered his alleged Roman origins "mere supposition."*

*See The Three Crowns of Florence: Humanist Assessments of
Dante, Petrarca and Boccaccio, ed. & trans. David Thompson and
Alan F. Nagel (to be published by Harper & Row).*

*From The Earliest Lives of Dante, translated from the Italian of
Giovanni Boccaccio and Leonardo Bruni Aretino by James Robinson Smith, Yale Studies in English, X (New York, 1901).*

DANTE'S BIRTH
(*Trattatello in Laude di Dante*, II)

FLORENCE, the noblest of Italian cities, had her beginning, as
ancient history and the general opinion of the present time seem to
declare, from the Romans. Increasing in size as years went on, and
filled with people and famous men, she began to appear to all her
neighbors not only as a city but a power. What the cause of change
was from these great beginnings—whether adverse fortune, or un-
favorable skies, or the deserts of her citizens—we cannot be sure. But
certain it is that, not many centuries later, Attila, that most cruel
king of the Vandals, and general spoiler of nearly all Italy, after he

had slain or dispersed all or the greater part of the citizens that were
known for their noble blood or for some other distinction, reduced
the city to ashes and ruins.

In this condition it is thought to have remained for more than
three hundred years. At the end of that period, the Roman Empire
having been transferred, and not without cause, from Greece to
Gaul, Charles the Great, then the most clement King of the French,
was raised to the imperial throne. At the close of many labors,
moved, as I believe, by the Divine Spirit, he turned his imperial
mind to the rebuilding of the desolated city. He it was who caused
it to be rebuilt and inhabited by members of the same families from
which the original founders were drawn, making it as far as possible
like to Rome. And although he reduced the circumference of the
walls, he nevertheless gathered within them the few descendants of
the ancient fugitives.

Now among the new inhabitants (perhaps, as fame attests, the
director of the rebuilding, allotter of the houses and streets, and
giver of wise laws to the new people) was one who came from Rome,
a most noble youth of the house of the Frangipani, whom everybody
called Eliseo. When he had finished the main work for which he
had come, he became, either from love of the city newly laid out by
him, or from the pleasantness of the site, to which he perceived perhaps that the skies were in the future to be propitious, or drawn on
by whatever other cause, a permanent citizen there. And the family
of children and descendants, not small, nor little to be praised, which
he left behind him, abandoned the ancient surname of their ancestors, and took in its stead the name of their founder in Florence,
and all called themselves the Elisei.

Among the other members of this family, as time went on and son
descended from father, there was born and there lived a knight by
the name of Cacciaguida, in arms and in judgment excellent and
brave.[1] In his youth his elders gave him for a bride a maiden born of
the Aldighieri of Ferrara, prized for her beauty and her character, no
less than for her noble blood. They lived together many years, and
had several children. Whatever the others may have been called, in
one of the children it pleased the mother to renew the name of her
ancestors—as women often are fond of doing—and so she called him

Aldighieri, although the word later, corrupted by the dropping of the "d," survived as Alighieri. The excellence of this man caused his descendants to relinquish the title Elisei, and take as their patronymic Alighieri; which name it holds to this day. From him were descended many children, grandchildren, and great-grandchildren; and, during the reign of Emperor Frederick II, an Alighieri was born who was destined, more through his son than of himself, to become famous. . . .

This [son] was that Dante of whom the present discourse treats. This was that Dante given to our age by the special grace of God. This was that Dante who was the first to open the way for the return of the Muses, banished from Italy. By him the glory of the Florentine idiom has been made manifest; by him all the beauties of the vulgar tongue have been set to fitting numbers; by him dead poesy may truly be said to have been revived. . . . This special glory of Italy was born in our city in the year of the saving incarnation of the King of the universe 1265, when the Roman Empire was without a ruler owing to the death of the aforesaid Frederick, and Pope Urban the Fourth was sitting in the chair of Saint Peter.[2]

[1] See Dante, *Paradiso* XV-XVII.
[2] The pope at that time was actually Clement IV.

LEONARDO BRUNI

The Praise of the City of Florence was composed in 1403/1404, to celebrate the city's survival in the wars against Giangaleazzo Visconti's Milanese tyranny. (Bruni's panegyric imitates Aristides' Panathenaicus, which had praised Athens for saving Greece from Persian despotism.) As an initiate to Florence's Guelph tradition, Bruni stood opposed not to Roman imperialism but to the Roman Empire, to any rule by one man, which he saw as the end of republican intellectual and political vitality.

On Salutati, Bruni and the re-assessment of Roman and Floren-

tine history, see Hans Baron, The Crisis of the Early Italian Renaissance, rev. one-vol. ed. (Princeton, 1966), esp. chapter 3. The following excerpts have been translated from the first complete edition, in
Hans Baron, From Petrarch to Leonardo Bruni (Chicago & London,
1968), a volume which also contains two studies of the Laudatio.

FLORENCE, THE HEIR OF REPUBLICAN ROME
(Laudatio Florentinae Urbis)

HOW valuable it is, that Florentines descend from the Roman
people! What nation in the whole world was ever more glorious,
more powerful, more distinguished for every sort of virtue than the
Roman people? Its exploits are so illustrious that in comparison the
greatest deeds of other men seem mere child's play; its empire, co-
extensive with the earth, was so well governed through many centuries that more examples of valor stand forth from that one city
than were produced in the whole history of all other republics—a
city in which there stood forth innumerable men of so extraordinary
valor that none were ever equal to them on earth. For to say nothing of other pre-eminently great commanders and leading men of
the senate, where in the world outside the city of Rome will you find
a Publicola, a Fabricius, the Coruncani, the Dentati, the Fabii, the
Decii, the Camilli, the Paulli, the Marcelli, the Scipios, the Catos,
the Gracchi, the Torquati, a Cicero? And if you seek renown in a
founder, you could find nothing in the whole world more renowned
than the Roman people; if riches, nothing more wealthy; if grandeur
and magnificence, nothing more brilliant and glorious: within
Ocean's waters there is nothing which was not subdued by arms and
in their power. Wherefore to you also, men of Florence, lordship of
the earth belongs by a sort of hereditary right, like the possession of
a patrimony. From this it also follows that all wars waged by the
Florentine people are completely just, and that in waging wars this
people cannot lack justice, since perforce it wages all its wars for the
defence or recovery of its own property—which two types of war are
permitted by all systems of law.

· · ·

This most illustrious colony of the Romans was established at
precisely the time when the empire of the Roman people was most
flourishing, when the most powerful kings and most warlike nations
had been vanquished by their military valor: Carthage, Numantia,
and Corinth had perished root and branch; every land and every sea
had come into the power of this people; no calamity had been inflicted on the Roman people by any foe. Not yet had liberty been
done away with by the likes of Caesar, Antony, Tiberius, Nero—
banes and ruinations of the republic. Liberty was in its bloom, in-
violable and unshaken; but wicked robbers took it away soon after
the founding of this colony. On this account, I believe, there came
about what we see to have been, and to be, the case in this state
singularly beyond others: that the men of Florence rejoice most of
all in liberty and are vehemently hostile to tyrants. From that time,
in my opinion, Florence conceived such hatred for the invaders of
the empire and subverters of the republic that not even today does
it seem to have forgotten: if any name or trace of them still remains,
this republic scorns and hates it.

· · ·

For what indignation was ever more just? Or who was more
touched by that grief than the Florentine people, when they saw the
Roman people, their parent and founder—which a little while before
ruled every land, vanquished by their great valor—deprived of its
own liberty and torn to pieces by utterly vicious men who, were
the republic strong, would have been among its lowest dregs? . . .
What has ever been seen or heard more repulsive, more disgraceful,
than the barbarities Tiberius devised on Capri in torturing and
destroying Roman citizens? Or the little fishes and male prostitutes
of the same emperor, abominable and unheard-of types of wanton-
ness?[1] It seems to me a disgrace for Italy that such shameful acts
once took place in it.

But if these emperors were completely repulsive and pernicious,
nevertheless those who followed afterwards were better. Who, pray
tell? Nero, I suppose, and Vitellius and Domitian and Heliogabalus?
To be sure. For it's hard to say what great virtue and humanity

Nero possessed. His mother Agrippina with wondrous praises exalts to heaven her son's piety; and he who showed such piety toward his mother is not to be thought impious and unkind toward others: compassion even led him—so that his fellow-citizens should not be hurt by the cold—to burn the city itself.

---

[1] Cf. Suetonius, *Life of Tiberius* 43-44. Neither the Bohn nor the Loeb translator, though, could bring himself to render it all into English.

MACHIAVELLI

The greatest work of Florence's greatest political writer took the form of Discourses upon the First Decade of Livy; and in all Machiavelli's writings the actions of the Romans remained his touchstone, his standard of political wisdom.

The History of Florence was commissioned in 1520 by Cardinal Giulio de' Medici, then head of the University of Florence; and when Machiavelli had carried the story down to the death of Lorenzo he went to Rome to present it to his patron, who was by then Pope Clement VII. This was Machiavelli's last important literary work, for he died in 1527, the same year Rome was sacked by the troops of Charles V, the Holy Roman Emperor.

See Federico Chabod, Machiavelli and the Renaissance, trans. David Moore (London, 1958; also re-issued as a Harper Torchbook); Felix Gilbert, Machiavelli and Guicciardini (Princeton, 1965); and Roberto Ridolfi, The Life of Niccolò Machiavelli (Chicago, 1963). For support of Charles' action: Alfonso de Valdés and the Sack of Rome: Dialogue of Lactancio and an Archdeacon, ed. and trans. John E. Longhurst with the collaboration of Raymond R. Mac-Curdy (Albuquerque, 1952).

From The History of Florence and of the Affairs of Italy . . . (London: Bell, 1891).

THE DOMESTIC DISCORDS OF REPUBLICS
(*History of Florence* III, Ch. I)

THOSE serious, though natural enmities, which occur between the
popular classes and the nobility, arising from the desire of the latter
to command, and the disinclination of the former to obey, are the
causes of most of the troubles which take place in cities; and from
this diversity of purposes, all the other evils which disturb republics
derive their origin.[1] This kept Rome disunited; and this, if it be
allowable to compare small things with great,[2] held Florence in dis-
union; although in each city it produced a different result; for
animosities were only beginning when the people and nobility of
Rome contended, whilst ours were brought to a conclusion by the
contentions of our citizens. A new law settled the disputes of Rome;
those of Florence were only terminated by the death and banishment of many of her best people. Those of Rome increased her
military virtue, whilst that of Florence was quite extinguished by her
divisions. The quarrels of Rome established different ranks of society, those of Florence abolished the distinctions which had previously existed. This diversity of effects must have been occasioned
by the different purposes which the two people had in view. Whilst
the people of Rome endeavored to associate with the nobility in the
supreme honors, those of Florence strove to exclude the nobility
from all participation in them: as the desire of the Roman people
was more reasonable, no particular offence was given to the nobility;
they therefore consented to it without having recourse to arms; so
that, after some disputes concerning particular points, both parties
agreed to the enactment of a law which, while it satisfied the people,
preserved the nobility in the enjoyment of their dignity.

On the other hand, the demands of the people of Florence being
insolent and unjust, the nobility became desperate, prepared for
their defence with their utmost energy, and thus bloodshed and the
exile of citizens followed. The laws which were afterwards made did
not provide for the common good, but were framed wholly in favor
of the conquerors. This too must be observed, that from the acquisition of power made by the people of Rome, their minds were very

much improved; for all the offices of state being attainable as well by the people as the nobility, the peculiar excellencies of the latter exercised a most beneficial influence upon the former; and as the city increased in virtue she attained a more exalted greatness.

But in Florence, the people being conquerors, the nobility were deprived of all participation in the government; and, in order to regain a portion of it, it became necessary for them not only to seem like the people, but to be like them in behavior, mind, and mode of living. Hence arose those changes in armorial bearings, and in the titles of families, which the nobility adopted, in order that they might seem to be of the people; military virtue and generosity of feeling became extinguished in them; the people not possessing these qualities, they could not appreciate them, and Florence became by degrees more and more depressed and humiliated. The virtue of the Roman nobility degenerating into pride, the citizens soon found that the business of the state could not be carried on without a prince. Florence had now come to such a point, that with a comprehensive mind at the head of affairs she would easily have been made to take any form that he might have been disposed to give her; as may be partly observed by a perusal of the preceding book. . . .

---

1 The first part of the *History* focuses on domestic events, especially the civil strife which Machiavelli felt had been almost ignored by his predecessors, Bruni and Poggio (on whom see Donald J. Wilcox, *The Development of Florentine Humanist Historiography in the Fifteenth Century*, Harvard Historical Studies, 82 [Cambridge, Mass., 1969]).

2 Cf. Virgil, *Eclogue* I, 23.

BIBLIOGRAPHY

Books and articles in English, treating particular aspects of our topic, have been cited in the notes on individual texts. Some books of general scope are:

1. Chester G. Starr, *The Emergence of Rome as Ruler of the Western World* (Ithaca, 1950).
2. E. K. Rand, *The Building of Eternal Rome* (Cambridge, Mass., 1943).
3. *The Legacy of Rome*, ed. Cyril Bailey (Oxford, 1923).

Three major works in foreign languages, which together encompass most of our material, are:

1. Friedrich Klingner, *Römische Geisteswelt* (Munich, 1956).
2. Francois Paschoud, *Roma Aeterna, Études sur le Patriotisme Romain dans l'Occident Latin a l'Époque des Grandes Invasions* (Institut Suisse de Rome, 1957).
3. Arturo Graf, *Roma nella Memoria e nelle Immaginazioni del Medio Evo*, new edition (Turin, 1923).

There are good paperback editions of many of the writers included in this volume, among them:

1. Polybius, *The Histories* (abridged), trans. M. Chambers, ed. E. Badian (Washington Square Press).
2. Cicero, *On the Commonwealth*, trans. G. H. Sabine and S. B. Smith (Bobbs-Merrill).
3. Sallust, *Jugurthine War; Conspiracy of Catiline*, trans. S. A. Handford (Penguin).
4. Livy, *The Early History of Rome*, trans. A. de Sélincourt (Penguin).
5. Mommsen, *History of Rome* (abridged), eds. D. A. Saunders and J. H. Collins, rev. ed. (Meridian).
6. Virgil, *Aeneid*, trans. F. O. Copley (Bobbs-Merrill).
7. Saint Luke, *The Acts of the Apostles*, trans. C. H. Rieu (Penguin).

8. Tacitus, *Complete Works*, trans. A. J. Church and W. J. Brodribb, ed. Moses Hadas (Modern Library).

9. *The Portable Gibbon*, ed. D. A. Saunders (Viking).

10. Saint Augustine, *The City of God* (abridged), ed. V. J. Bourke, introd. E. Gilson (Doubleday).

11. Bryce, *The Holy Roman Empire*, introd. Hans Kohn (Schocken).

12. *The Portable Dante*, ed. P. Milano (Viking).

13. *Petrarch: A Humanist among Princes*, ed. David Thompson (Harper).

14. Boccaccio and Bruni, *The Earliest Lives of Dante* (Ungar).

15. Machiavelli, *History of Florence*, introd. Felix Gilbert (Harper).

16. Burckhardt, *The Civilization of the Renaissance in Italy*, ed. Irene Gordon (Mentor).